Debra Shipley and Mary Peplow are freelance journalists working in both broadcasting and the national press. Their interests are wide and varied, ranging from parks to pageantry, culture to crafts, drawing to jogging.

D0620351

By the same authors

London For Free
The London Fun Book
Edinburgh For Free
Dublin For Free
Glasgow For Free
Tube Trails
The Other Museum Guide

AROUND THE EDGE OF IRELAND

Debra Shipley
and
Mary Peplow

GRAFTON BOOKS

A Division of the Collins Publishing Group

LONDON GLASGOW
TORONTO SYDNEY AUCKLAND

Grafton Books
A Division of the Collins Publishing Group
8 Grafton Street, London WIX 3LA

A Grafton Paperback Original 1990

Copyright © Debra Shipley and
Mary Peplow 1990

A CIP catalogue record for this book
is available from the British Library

ISBN 0-586-20633-7

Printed and bound in Great Britain by
Collins, Glasgow

Set in Galliard

CONTENTS

ACKNOWLEDGEMENTS

On our journey around the edge of Ireland we met and were helped by many people and we'd like to thank them all for both their friendly encouragement and all the useful information they gave us. We'd particularly like to thank Chuck and Margaret Evans and their son Peter, Tom and Olive Witherow from Newcastle, Simon Molesworth, Richard and Emma Atkinson, Peter and Jennifer Rohde, and Marian Manley.

The tourist boards in both the north and south continually pointed us in the right direction and our thanks especially to John Lahiffe, Tim Magennis, Philippa Reid, Mark Rowlett, Jack Walsh.

Finally, we must say a big thank you to our commissioning editor, Ian Paten and Grafton's former Irish rep., Jim Lowth – we couldn't have even started the project without them!

Debra Shipley and Mary Peplow

INTRODUCTION

Around the Edge of Ireland is a record of our journey around Ireland's coastline. We have tried to record things we saw and places we visited in our own personal way; these are very much our individual impressions. Although Ireland has a timeless quality the atmosphere of the places mentioned does tend to change. A tranquil picnic spot with a panoramic view one day might be a windswept promontory the next. The weather can be a major factor in enjoying touring in Ireland. It's frequently wet, overcast or drizzly, especially in the west. It's best to expect poor weather and you may be pleasantly surprised; better still, enjoy the rain! We found that whenever we travelled, winter and summer, we needed our waterproofs and wellington boots.

We used a selection of maps but found it most useful to have one map of the whole of Ireland and then a selection of more detailed local maps. Even so, some places were hard to find and at times even more difficult to leave; near the coast, roads often deteriorate into a maze of tiny lanes. We also had some problems with signposts, particularly in the rural areas. We discovered that places sometimes have numerous names and we have our doubts about the accuracy of distances.

During our research we stayed in a wide variety of accommodation, including farmhouses, bed and breakfast, hotels, country houses and campsites. Their prices and quality varied enormously. However, we are both agreed that undoubtedly our best experience was travelling and sleeping in a motorhome. These are of course welcome on camp and caravan sites but many farmers if asked politely will let you park on their land either for a small fee or completely free.

For convenience we have started our guide to the edge of Ireland at

County Dublin and have commenced clockwise around its coastline. We have organized the book into sixteen sections representing the counties which have substantial sections of coastline. For each we have provided a short introduction and a selection of some of the places we enjoyed. The accompanying maps should be used in conjunction with more detailed road maps; they are merely to show that it's worth looking out for something. Similarly, our practical information is meant only as an indication.

We are sure we have missed out things so if you come across anywhere which you'd like to recommend please drop us a line and tell us about it. If you want to know more about places of interest, accommodation, travel details, restaurants and activities such as angling and golf, contact: Irish Tourist Board (Bord Fáilte), Baggot Street Bridge, Dublin 2. Tel: (01) – 0001 from outside the country – 765871 or the Northern Ireland Tourist Board, River House, 48 High Street, Belfast BT1 2DS. Tel: (0232) 231221. These are the head offices but you'll also find a number of tourist information points throughout Ireland, some of which have seasonal opening times.

AROUND
THE EDGE OF
IRELAND

COUNTY DUBLIN

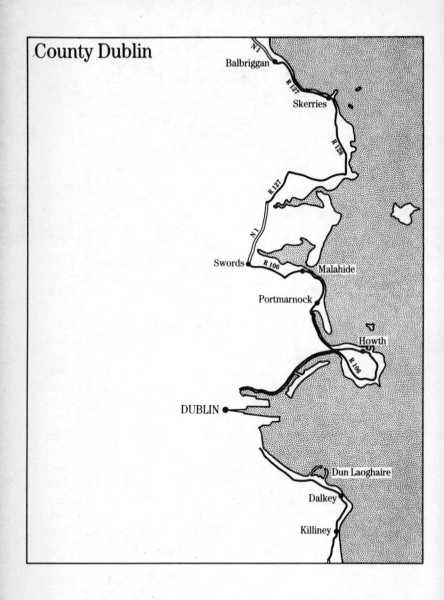

County Dublin

Balbriggan

N1

R 127

Skerries

R 128

R 127

N1

Swords
R 106
Malahide

Portmarnock

Howth

R 106

DUBLIN

Dun Laoghaire

Dalkey

Killiney

COUNTY DUBLIN

Dublin City, once a Viking settlement and now the Republic's capital city and principal port, spreads over the bulk of the county. The city is beautifully set on the sweep of Dublin Bay where the River Liffey, which rises in the Dublin Mountains, flows out into the sea. The much-loved Liffey runs through the centre of Dublin, neatly dividing it into north and south. It is the rather murky peat-coloured water of this river which gave Dublin its name – Duiblinn, or Dark Pool.

To the north of the city is the peninsula of Howth, which for travellers heading northwards heralds the start of a low and rolling coastline of long sandy beaches, fishing harbours and well-kept picture postcard villages. On the southern shore of Dublin Bay is Dun Laoghaire, the busy terminus for the ferry from Holyhead. The coast road leads southwards to the headland of Dalkey then skirts the lovely Killiney Bay to the popular seaside resort of Bray.

Inland and north of the city the wooded slopes of the Dublin Mountains make fine walking country. The Wicklow Way, the first long-distance footpath in the Republic, begins at Marlay Park and runs for around 132 km taking walkers over the eastern flanks of the sparsely populated Dublin and Wicklow Mountains, the largest unbroken area of high ground in Ireland. From Marlay the route climbs to around 300 m on the Kilmashogue Forest Trail offering panoramic views of the city of Dublin and its surrounding countryside. To the north the peaks of the Mourne Mountains can be seen far away in County Down, and much nearer to the south, stand the gentle Wicklow Mountains.

BALBRIGGAN

A small seaside town, Balbriggan, 32 km north of Dublin, is a charming introduction to the county. Quiet and unspoilt, it doesn't boast many leisure amenities or places of particular interest, just a sheltered sandy beach set in delightful scenery. However, it does have some historical importance, for the well-stocked trout river, the River Devlin, is said to be the christening site of St Benignus, successor to St Patrick. The small manufacturing town is probably best known for making stockings. Some people still call them balbriggans.

SKERRIES

The dry, bracing air at this seaside resort is quite something. Refreshing and invigorating, Skerries, with its long sweeping beach, is the place where many Dubliners come to get away from the hustle and bustle of the big city. The name Skerries is Norse, a reference to the three islands offshore. Stand on the pier and you'll get a good view of these rocky islands: St Patrick's Island, Colt Island and Shenick's Island with its Martello tower. St Patrick's Island is named after St Patrick, who is said to have built the church which now stands in ruins on the island. He is believed to have begun his mission from here, travelling over to Red Island, now part of the mainland, where his 'footprints' can be seen in the rock. When the tide is low you can walk over to Shenick's Island, but you must hire a boat to reach the other two.

Looking northwest from the pier you can see Rockabill Lighthouses, a lonely sight in the midst of the Irish Sea; and to the southeast is Lambay Island, where the Vikings are said to have first landed. With a good pair of binoculars you can spot the different species of seabirds that breed around Lambay Island.

Skerries is set in idyllic countryside for walking. Bernageragh Bay is a popular picnic spot while a cliff path leads southwards to Loughshinny, an unspoilt fishing village with a tiny harbour and hotch-potch of houses.

MALAHIDE CASTLE
Malahide

Malahide is an attractive harbour town where the people obviously take great pride in appearance. The gardens are all neatly laid out, not a thing is out of place. It comes as no surprise that this village on the south side of the Broadwater estuary, famed for its fascinating fossils, has won many awards for its tidiness.

Malahide is best known for its castle, which was until recently the home of the Talbot family, a residence that had lasted for nearly 800 years, interrupted only for a short time during the Cromwellian invasion. The romantic castle has seen many alterations over the years and also played host to a fascinating array of personalities. It was here, for example, that the diaries of James Boswell were first found in a croquet box; and here, in the Church of St Sylvester, that Maud Plunket was buried, 'Maid, wife and widow in one day.'

Several of the lavishly furnished rooms are open to the public. The Oak Room is covered in richly carved panelling. Of particular note is the Flemish carving of the Coronation of the Virgin, which dates back to the sixteenth century. The medieval Great Hall, although rather gloomy today, was the scene of many a gay and sumptuous banquet. Dominating the room is the huge painting of the Battle of the Boyne by Jan Wyck, dated 1693, only three years after the momentous battle. The Talbots were followers of James II and it's said that at least fourteen family members sat down to breakfast in the Great Hall on the morning of the bloody contest, never to return.

The castle is home to much of the National Portrait Collection from the National Gallery (see page 20) and many of the paintings hang in the Great Hall. Faces of the Talbot family line the walls, complemented by portraits of eminent figures and people who have played a part in the history of Ireland and the castle, including a portrait of James Gandon, the Dublin architect, and a self-portrait of Nathaniel Hone the Elder. The castle grounds include a large botanic garden with 5,000 different species and varieties of plants, all meticulously labelled.

The Fry Model Railway Museum is in the castle grounds, the first of its kind in Ireland. All railway buffs will be interested by the model trains, trams and railway artefacts.

Malahide Castle. Tel: (01) 452337
Open: all year, Mon–Fri,
10.00–17.00 (closed 12.45–14.00);
Apr–Oct (inc), Sat, 11.00–18.00;
Sun and Bank Hols, 14.00–18.00;
Nov–Mar (inc), Sat, Sun and Bank
Hols, 14.00–17.00
Admission charge

Railway Museum
Open: Apr–Oct, Mon–Thurs,
10.00–13.00, 14.00–17.00; Sat,
11.00–13.00, 14.00–18.00; Sun,
14.00–18.00; Nov–Mar,
Mon–Thurs, 10.00–13.00,
14.00–17.00; Sat, Sun and Bank
Hols, 14.00–17.00; closed Fri
Admission charge

HOWTH

If you're planning to spend a day in Howth, then do stay on for the evening's entertainment. Sample the delights of traditional Irish music at the world-renowned Abbey Tavern (reservations essential). And at about 18.30, before the music starts, the large fishing fleet comes in with its delicious catch up for sale around the colourful harbour (Thursday evening is the best time to see all the action). Howth, a name derived from the Norse 'hoved' or head, is a pretty village of steep streets on the southern shore of Howth peninsula. A dramatic cliff walk takes you from Balscadden around the peninsula to the Bailey Lighthouse. The route is not difficult, but you will need to allow yourself plenty of time to enjoy it to the full.

Howth Castle, much altered over the years but still lived in by descendants of the St Lawrence family who first built it in 1464, is another landmark of the area. It also has an interesting tale attached to it. Legend has it that Grace O'Malley, the 'Pirate Queen', stopped off at Howth Castle asking for food and shelter but was refused. Furious, she captured the son and heir and took him back with her to County Mayo. He was only released after the family promised that hungry travellers would never be turned away. The present family still keeps up the tradition of laying an extra place at the table.

The castle isn't open to the public, but you can wander around the grounds, famed for their spectacular show of over 2,000 rhododendrons that burst into vivid colour in May and June. Although rich in horticultural interest, it's worth visiting these hilly grounds just for the views. From here you can see out to Ireland's Eye and Lambay

Island to the north, and to the west the long, low Bull Island, now a bird sanctuary.

Abbey Tavern. Tel: (01) 322006
Open: summer, nightly except Sun; winter, varies
Cover charge (reservations essential)

Howth Castle Gardens. Tel: (01) 322624
Open: all year, daily 08.00–sunset
Admission charge

DUBLIN
Tourist Information: 14 Upper O'Connell Street.
Tel: (01) 747733

Dublin was first noted on a map in 140 AD named Eblana after the tribe who once occupied the area. However, the city recognizes its true origins in the Viking settlement which began in 988 AD around the recently excavated Wood Quay and grew into an important trading port.

Dublin celebrated its millennium in 1988. A thousand years of turbulent history were marked by special events and festivals and also a much-needed programme of cleaning and renovating the main buildings and monuments. Dublin is notoriously dark and dull, known affectionately by locals as 'dear, dirty Dublin', but efforts during the millennium year have at least gone some way to brightening up the buildings. The millennium also brought a new and much talked about resident to one of the city's main shopping streets. In the centre of O'Connell Street there is now a statue of Anna Livia, goddess of the River Liffey, or the 'floozy in the jacuzzi' as some Dubliners jokingly call the figure in the fountain.

Dublin is small and compact by international standards; all the places of interest are within a short distance of each other. It is most definitely a city to discover on foot, not only because the parking is so poor and the streets so congested, but also because much of the charm of Dublin is found not in its history, its old churches or its elegant Georgian buildings, but in the friendliness of the people. And it is only by exploring the side streets and calling in for a drink in one of the packed pubs or for a coffee at the famous Bewley's cafés that you really appreciate their warmth and wit.

Abbey Theatre, Lower Abbey Street, Dublin 1. Tel: (01) 787222. Dublin's premier theatre, the Abbey, can tell a story as entertaining as the many plays it presents each year. Opened in 1904, it became a major venue for works by Irish playwrights. Three years later, J. M. Synge's highly controversial *Playboy of the Western World* provoked riots from the nationalist audience. There was more rioting in 1926 during the first performance of Sean O'Casey's *The Plough and the Stars*.

An evening at the Abbey is an altogether more peaceful affair these days. Indeed, although its aim is still to produce Irish plays by Irish authors, commercial pressures have forced it to widen its appeal to cater for a popular audience. The original theatre was burned down in 1951 and was replaced by the present rather stark modern building, which also houses the small Peacock Theatre, noted for its experimental plays.

For performance details contact the Box Office.

Guinness Brewery, St James's Gate, Dublin 8. Tel: (01) 536700. Think of Ireland and pleasant thoughts of its dark, creamy brew immediately come to mind. Guinness, one of Ireland's favourite drinks, is brewed here at St James's Gate. You can't miss it – the distinct smell will direct you! The brewery does not offer guided tours but visitors are shown an audio-visual presentation outlining the history of the Guinness family and given a glossy brochure as a souvenir. And to send you away in good spirits, there's a free glass of the 'sublime porter' as James Joyce described Guinness. The brewery is popular and a visit is all rather rushed, but it's very much part of a trip to the city.

Open: all year, Mon–Fri,
10.00–15.00 (no need to book)
Admission free

National Gallery of Ireland, Merrion Square West. Tel: (01) 615133. By national gallery standards, Ireland's is perhaps small, but it does have a reasonable Dutch collection and a number of works by painters from the Spanish, French and Italian schools. Unsurprisingly, it also has an exceptionally good collection of works by Irish painters, most notably paintings by Jack Yeats. If you don't know very much about Irish paintings it's a good idea to join a free guided tour.

Open: Mon–Fri, 10.00–18.00;   **Admission free**
(Thurs until 21.00); Sun,
13.00–17.00

National Museum, Kildare Street. Tel: (01) 765521. This is a wonderful place to see some of Ireland's real treasures like the Tara Brooch and the Ardagh Chalice. They are both Celtic treasures, but the remains housed in the National Museum trace Ireland's history from around 6000 BC to the present. There are some beautiful glass and lace pieces, and in contrast the evocative blood-stained vest once worn by James Connolly, along with some of the finest early Christian art to be found in Europe.

Open: Tues–Sat, 10.00–17.00;
Sun, 14.00–17.00
Admission free

Phoenix Park, Dublin 7. Tel: (01) 213021. Only an aerial view of Dublin can illustrate the vastness of this great park just a short bus ride away from the city centre. Green and leafy, the park covers some 1,760 acres and unless you've got a good sense of direction it's easy to get gloriously lost, so take care or rather take a good map! One of the more unusual features of the park is that it plays host to polo matches during the summer season. The matches are always well supported and the quick and skilful play is fun to watch.

The park also offers the chance to see a game of Gaelic football or hurling in the sports area of the park, called the Fifteen Acres, where a million people gathered in 1979 to hear Pope John Paul II say Mass. The flower-filled People's Gardens, by the Park Gate entrance, stand in the shadow of the Wellington Monument, one of Dublin's best-known landmarks. This massive statue, which towers to a height of 205 feet, was designed in 1817 to commemorate Wellington's battles. In the centre of the park there's another monument, a statue of a phoenix known as the Phoenix Column, which stands beside a natural spring. The Irish for the clear water from the spring is 'Fionn Usice', pronounced by the English as phoenix – hence the name of the park.

The park was once a royal deer park and deer still wander freely. It is also home for Dublin's zoological gardens, famed for their lions.

Park
Open: all the time

People's gardens
Open: all year, Mon–Sat from 10.30, Sun from 10.00; closes Jan and Dec 16.00, Feb and Nov 17.00, Mar 18.00, Oct 19.00, Apr and Sept 20.00, May and Aug 21.00, Jan and July 21.30
Admission free

St Patrick's Cathedral, Patrick Street, Dublin 8. Tel: (01) 536700. Huge and impressive, St Patrick's, one of the largest cathedrals in Ireland, dates mainly from the thirteenth century. Over the years the building has suffered its fair share of traumas: fire, desecration, neglect – it was even used to stable the horses of Cromwell's troops – but restoration work has helped preserve its beauty, fine monuments and stained-glass windows. The cathedral has close links with Jonathan Swift, satirist and author, best known for *Gulliver's Travels*, who was Dean of the Cathedral 1713–45. There's a corner devoted to Swift and, above a doorway in the south aisle, his epitaph, written by Swift himself, in Latin.

Next to St Patrick's is Archbishop Marsh's Library, reached by a small garden scented with sweet-smelling herbs. The library, with its dark oak bookcases lined with leather-bound books, was built by Archbishop Marsh in the early eighteenth century. It was the first lending library in Ireland and intended for the improvement of 'all graduates and gentlemen'. Books are no longer on loan but it still has all the trappings of a scholars' library.

Cathedral
Open: Mon–Fri, 09.00–18.00; Sat, 09.00–16.00
Admission free (donations welcome in the cathedral)

Library. Tel: (01) 753917
Open: all year, Mon, 14.00–16.00; Wed–Fri, 10.30–12.30, 14.00–16.00; Sat, 10.30–12.30

St Stephen's Green, Dublin 2. Right in the heart of the city just off Grafton Street, the fashionable shopping street, is an unusual and very pleasant sight – a beautiful park. Laid out in 1880 as a public park at the expense of Lord Ardilaun (Sir Arthur Guinness 1840–1915), it is still a popular place to sit or picnic – and a favourite place to feed ducks. Standing in the northeast corner is a memorial to Theobald Wolfe Tone, a harrowing portrayal of a desperate family living in poverty in the late eighteenth century. On a happier note, there's an ornamental lake, a waterfall and many lovingly maintained flower beds. A special feature of the green is the garden for blind people where all the plants are labelled in braille.

Open: all year, Mon–Sat,
08.00–dark; Sun, 10.00–dark
Admission free

Trinity College and the Book of Kells, College Street, Dublin 2. Tel: (01) 772941. If you see nothing else in Dublin, don't miss the Book of Kells, housed in the Old Library at Trinity College. Much-visited and much-photographed, it is one of the most beautiful and most celebrated illuminated manuscripts in the world. There are two volumes on display, one opened at an illuminated page, the other at a page of text. Full of symbolism and intricate detailing, the book, which tells the story of Christ, was produced by talented monks and is said to date from as early as 800 AD. You will probably have to join a long queue to see the manuscript but it's well worth the wait.

Trinity College itself was founded in 1591 by Queen Elizabeth I of England and is still a thriving university. Several of its buildings, set around a cobbled courtyard, are open to the public and there is much of interest to see. The courtyard, viewed by thousands as the setting for the film *Educating Rita*, is dominated by the bell tower said to mark the centre of the original priory church. Beyond the tower is a row of buildings known as Rubrics, which are the oldest surviving part of the college and date from the early eighteenth century. Just to the right of these red houses is the Old Library, a magnificent room in its own right although rather overshadowed by its famous treasure. The Examination Room boasts an ornamented plasterwork Adam ceiling and an organ said to have been taken from a Spanish ship in

1702, while the College Chapel is a quiet retreat from the bustle of students and tourists.

Open: all year, Mon–Fri,
09.30–16.45; Sat, 09.30–12.45
Admission charge

DUN LAOGHAIRE
Tourist Information: St Michael's Wharf. Tel: (01) 806984/5/6

Named after a fortress built here in the fifth century by Leary, High King of Ireland, Dun Laoghaire (pronounced Dunleary) is a popular seaside resort and busy ferry terminus. The town itself is rather spoilt by a modern shopping centre right in the middle but it still has some interesting side streets and a certain Victorian charm. The lovely harbour is fun to explore. As you can see from a map, the two piers, both over a mile long, form a horseshoe shape to shelter the harbour. They were built by the Scots engineer John Rennie (1817–52) and once made Dun Laoghaire the largest port in the world. The piers, both headed with unmanned lighthouses, have tremendous character. The West Pier is wild and windswept while the East Pier plays host to band recitals in the summer months.

East Pier is the starting point for a scenic walk along the Marine Parade to Sandycove Harbour and the Martello tower where James Joyce once stayed as the guest of Oliver St John Gogarty. The tower, now a museum devoted to Joyce, features in the opening scene of *Ulysses*, his most famous work. Full of items related to Joyce, including manuscripts and musical instruments, it's an interesting way of finding out more about the Dublin-born novelist.

Just opposite the tower is an extraordinary spot. Known as the Forty Foot, it is, much to the fury of opposing factions, a gentlemen-only bathing place. Even in the chilly winter months, gentlemen brave the waters in their birthday suits! The coastal road takes you a mile and a half on to Dalkey, a secluded and rather sleepy village with narrow winding streets and ancient buildings. A little further on is Killiney Hill Park. From its highest point there are marvellous views of the surrounding countryside. A short walk away is Vico Road, overlooking Killiney Bay. The bay is so often likened to the Bay of Naples that the roads and houses have all been given Italian names.

Joyce Museum. Tel: (01) 808571
Open: Apr–Oct, Mon–Sat,
10.00–13.00, 14.00–17.00; Sun,
14.30–18.00; rest of year by
appointment only
Admission charge

Killiney Hill Park
Open: all the time
Admission free

COUNTY WICKLOW

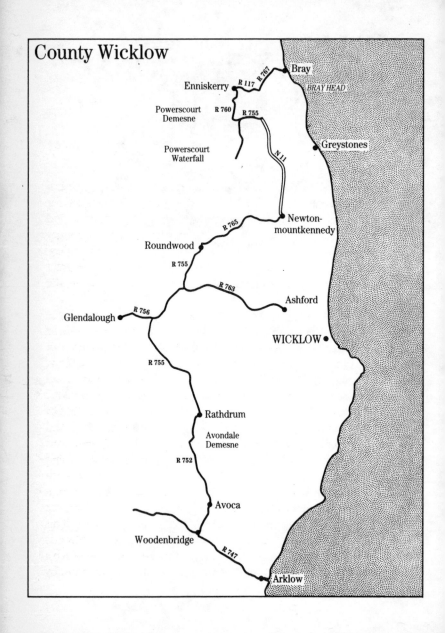

COUNTY WICKLOW

The County of Wicklow, just south of Dublin, has such diversity of scenery it has become known as the 'Garden of Ireland'. It is noted for its dramatic beauty, and there are quite breathtaking sights round every bend, making the roads a joy to drive. To the west of the county is a coastline of sandy beaches, inland are the fine lines of the Wicklow Mountains, which descend into the gentler plains around the great reservoir of Blessington and the valley of the Derry River in the east.

The coast road takes you through Wicklow, the county town on the lower slopes of Ballyguile Hill, over Wicklow Head with its three lighthouses, past the seaside resorts of Jack's Hole and Brittas Bay, out to Mizen Head and then down to the seaside town of Arklow. However, motorists are well advised to travel on a more scenic road slightly inland which crosses the domed granite Wicklow Mountains. Although known as mountains, these are more like hills, the highest of which, Lugnaquillia, is 927 m high. Their beauty is not wild and rugged but quite serene. Streams cascade from the high ground into the wooded valleys, and the slopes, decorated with golden gorse and purple heather, are studded with jewel-like tarns. The road leads through peat bogs, where turf is cut, to Glendalough, through Roundwood, reputed to be Ireland's highest village, and Clare, the smallest, to the vale of Avoca and the Meeting of the Waters. This famous spot where the Avonmore and Avonberg rivers meet is certainly picturesque but really there is little to warrant it being such a popular tourist attraction except, of course, the poetic description by Thomas Moore:

There is not in this wide world a valley so sweet
As that vale in whose blossom the bright waters meet;
Oh! The last rays of feeling and life must depart
Ere the bloom of that valley shall fade from my heart.

BRAY

Just 19 km south of Dublin, the coastal town of Bray has long been a seaside retreat for city dwellers in search of sand, sea and plenty of entertainment. The resort with its spacious strolling promenade reached a height of popularity in the nineteenth century when the coming of the railway made it easily accessible for a day or afternoon. For passing visitors today, however, the main attraction is Bray Head, which rises to some 237 m from the sea and, as you might expect, offers superb views.

The summit of Bray Head, where there are the ruins of a thirteenth-century church, can be reached in one of two ways. The path from the Greystones Road is fairly gentle. The Great White Way, which starts from the south end of the promenade, is much more exciting. The path winds steeply upwards taking you precariously close to the cliff's edge. Below you the sea splashes relentlessly against the shingle. Your efforts are well-rewarded once you reach the summit – on a clear day you can see as far out as Wales.

If you have time, a cliff walk runs from the eastern side of Bray Head along three miles of spectacular scenery and seascapes to the quiet resort and harbour town of Greystones.

POWERSCOURT ESTATE
Enniskerry. Tel: (01) 867676

On the outskirts of the pretty village of Enniskerry is the fairytale demesne of Powerscourt. The house, built around 1730, was sadly gutted by fire in 1974. Its shell, however, gives an indication of its former grandeur and provides a fitting backdrop to the numerous terraces, walks and formal gardens of the landscaped grounds. Stand in front of the burnt-out facade, looking down the flights of steps to the Triton Lake with its 18 m fountain, and there's an unrivalled view of the majestic Sugar Loaf Mountain, which rises to a height of 498 m.

From the house, tree-lined pathways lead to the intricate Japanese Garden, the Italianate Garden and Monkey Puzzle Avenue. There are also surprises such as a small Pet's Cemetery, a charming pepperpot tower and a stunning rhododendron and azalea walk. The gardens, which cover some 45 acres, are noted for their trees, some over 200 years old, but it's the statuary and ornamental gates that stay in your memory. Look out for the Bamberg Gate which came originally from the cathedral at Bamberg in Bavaria, dates from 1770 and guards the entrance to the gardens.

Nearby is the cascading Powerscourt Waterfall, the highest in Ireland, set scenically at the end of a long rhododendron drive. Water from the River Dargle tumbles almost vertically from a height of some 120 m into a winding stream, making an impressive spectacle. The area around the waterfall is lovely – perfect for walking and picnicking.

Gardens
Open: Mar–Oct, daily, 09.00–17.30
Admission charge

Waterfall
Open: all year, 10.30–19.00 (closes dusk in winter months)
Admission free

MOUNT USHER GARDENS
Ashford. Tel: (0404) 40116

The gardens at Mount Usher cover some 20 acres, mostly lining the banks of the River Vartry which flows through the centre. Pleasantly informal, with tree-lined walks, sparkling waterfalls and a collection of friendly ducks, it is a lovely place to roam and for the keen gardener there are a multitude of interesting plants to spot. As you wander around spare a thought for the humble beginnings of these gardens, now among the most famous in Ireland; they were first planted on a one-acre potato plot around an old cornmill! Started around 1870 by Edward Walpole, the gardens have developed under the supervision of leading horticultural experts over the years and today contain a vast number of trees and shrubs, many rare, some unique in Ireland, collected from all parts of the world.

The gardens are decked with flowers throughout the season. In spring the bulbs come to life spreading a flush of colour through the meadow areas. A little later you can expect to see fritillaries, dog's tooth violets, camellias and a spectacular display of rhododendrons. In May the rhododendrons are joined by a colourful mass of azaleas. June brings mock orange while July is the time to see the herbaceous plants at their best. August is marked by the appearance of California poppies and in September the hydrangeas and fuchsias are in bloom.

Determined not to rest on their laurels, the Walpole family, who still own the gardens, are continually expanding the gardens. Among the recent additions are a row of specialist shops and craft workshops where you can see a potter at work and visit a stained glass studio.

Open: mid-Mar – end Sept, Mon–Sat, 10.30–18.00; Sun, 11.00–18.00

Admission charge

GLENDALOUGH

The ruins here in the Valley of the Two Lakes are much photo-graphed, but it is one of those places that you must see with your own eyes to fully appreciate the beauty around you. Glendalough, set in scenic country with cool fresh air, spectacular views and the soothing sound of rippling water, is firmly on the 'beaten track'. During the summer the car park is packed with visitors. Thankfully, however, little can detract from its loveliness. Even when it is teeming with tourists, Glendalough is enchanting. On a bright spring day, the place is positively magical.

It was the quiet remoteness of its setting that first attracted St Kevin to the valley in the sixth century. A man who led a life of quiet meditation, he came in search of solitude and lived as a hermit, often sleeping, it's said, in the hollow of a tree. St Kevin left behind him a monastic city which later became a centre of learning and culture. His teachings were such an inspiration that a ninth-century bard, Aengus the Culdee, described the 'multitudinous Glendalough' as 'the Rome of the Western World'. Ruins scattered around the two lakes trace the history of the valley from St Kevin's early settlement to the dissolution of the monasteries at the Reformation. Each ruin has a plaque indicating its main features of historic and archaeological interest while the Visitor Centre in the main car park has imaginative displays and an audio-visual presentation.

The most important remains are to the east of the Lower Lake. Enter by a gateway next to the Royal Hotel. This was the original entrance to the monastic city that grew from St Kevin's first settlement. The largest and most eye-catching of the ruins is the cathedral. Dotted around the site are: St Kevin's Church, known as 'St Kevin's Kitchen'; the Round Tower, which is still in good condition; St Kevin's Cross, a plain granite structure dating back to the sixth or seventh century; the Priest's House within the ancient cemetery; St Ciaran's Church, named after the founder of Clonmacnois in County Offaly, another important Irish monastic site; and the twelfth-century St Saviour's Church, a mile east of the cathedral.

On the less easily accessible Upper Lake are: remains of some small stone huts, probably from a Bronze or early Iron Age fort; the ruined Reefert Church, a burial place for kings; and St Kevin's Cell, a beehive stone hut and place of refuge for St Kevin. There's a story that St Kevin was once sitting here in his cell when a blackbird swooped down and laid her eggs in his open hand. The saint stayed completely still until all the young birds had hatched.

Archaeological sites
Open: all the time
Admission free

Visitor Centre. Tel: (0404) 5352
Open: mid-June–mid-July,
10.00–17.00 daily;
mid-July–mid-Sept, 10.00–19.00
daily; mid-Sept–end Oct,
10.00–17.00 daily; Nov–mid-Mar,
Tues–Sat, 10.00–16.30; Sun,
14.30–16.30
Admission charge

AVONDALE HOUSE AND FOREST PARK
Rathdrum. Tel: (0404) 6111

One of Wicklow's more famous sons, the great social reformer Charles Stewart Parnell, was born at Avondale House, just south of Rathdrum, in 1846. The grand white house, built in 1779, is now a forestry school with some parts open to the public. Set up as a museum in honour of Parnell, it is actually rather stark inside and the contents are of limited appeal, a sharp contrast to the full and fascinating story of Parnell's life. Leader of the Irish Party in Westminster, he was one of the chief instigators of the campaign for land reform and the transfer of land from the landlords to the peasant farmers. Parnell died in 1891, his political career in tatters after a scandalous affair with Kitty O'Shea, but twelve years later his campaign finally achieved success with the Wyndham Land Act.

Avondale House is set in a forest park where the Forestry Service carry out research into trees and the conditions in which they prefer to grow. The park, which covers some 523 acres, mostly on the west bank of the River Avondale, is laid out with nature trails and picnic areas. Like so many of the beauty spots in Wicklow, it is certainly a sight for sore eyes but with so many different parts to explore, not for weary legs!

House
Open: May–Sept, Mon–Fri,
14.00–18.00

Park
Open: all year, daily
Admission charge: (car park only)

AVOCA HANDWEAVERS
Avoca. Tel: (0402) 5105

Here in the village of Avoca is the oldest handweaving mill still in use in Ireland. Records show that the mill was working as early as 1723. Farmers would bring their grain to be ground and their fleeces to be washed, spun and woven into cloth or blankets. The tradition continues for the mill is now the home of the Avoca Handweavers who specialize in pure wool and mohair products. The clothes, rugs, blankets, scarves and shawls, all in the heathery shades of the Wicklow Mountains, are a reminder of the days when mosses and lichens were used to dye the wool.

The centre is primarily a retail outlet with a craft shop and tea-room, but you are also welcome to watch the weavers at work. It all seems very primitive, but the old Fly Shuttle Loom they use does date back to the eighteenth century. It may appear slow by today's standards, but when it was first introduced workers were so fearful its fast production would put them out of a job that they started riots and loom burnings in protest. You can wander freely into the mill and talk to the weavers about the various processes, but guided tours are also available lasting around 15–20 minutes. The guide explains both about how the industry works and the individual skills and tremendous concentration needed to produce the intricately woven tweeds.

Mill
Open: all year, Mon–Fri, 08.00–16.30 (closed 13.00–13.30)
Admission free

Shop
Open: all year, Mon–Fri, 09.30–17.30; Sat and Sun, 10.00–17.30

ARKLOW

One of the main seaside resorts on the east coast, Arklow at the extreme south of the county is a good place for a shopping stop or refreshment break after a drive through the Wicklow Mountains. If time allows, there are some sandy beaches nearby too. The ancient town, made famous by its pottery, was once an important seaport and its strong maritime tradition is reflected in its small but interesting maritime museum. Boat building is still a local industry and the town takes credit for *Gypsy Moth II*, the yacht which Sir Francis Chichester sailed around the world. You may not want to stay long, but this town is worth a visit if only for its lovely location at the mouth of the River Avoca.

Maritime Museum, St Mary's Road. Tel: (0402) 32686

Open: May–Sept, 10.00–13.00 and 14.00–17.00
Admission charge

COUNTY WEXFORD

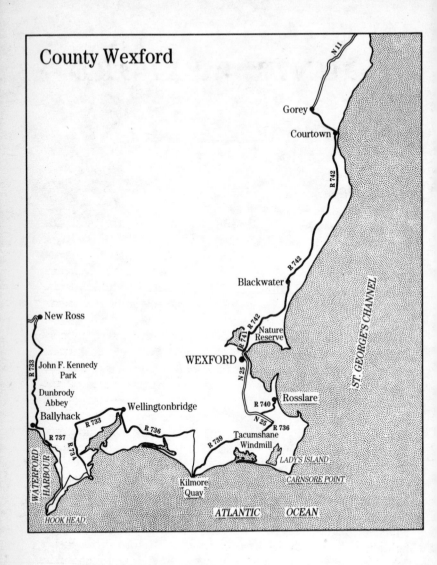

COUNTY WEXFORD

County Wexford is in the corner of Ireland known as the sunny southeast. And it's not just a publicity stunt – it's a fact that there are more hours of sunshine recorded at Rosslare, the busy ferry port, than anywhere else in Ireland. The county, which is divided by the River Slaney, is enclosed by natural borders: to the north are the hills of County Wicklow, to the west the River Barrow and the Blackstairs Mountains, while the Irish Sea laps the east coast and the Atlantic Ocean lies to the south. It is a county of low hills and scenic valleys with a coastline edged by long strands.

County Wexford has a long and turbulent history, its location so close to Europe making it a natural landing place for invading tribes, first the Neolithic peoples, then the Celts, the Vikings and the Normans. It was here, in 1169, that the Normans landed on the beaches of Baginbun and Bannow to begin their sweep through the country, building strong castles at strategic points and introducing a new system of local government to Ireland. The most influential Norman families were the Butlers and the Fitzgeralds, names which are still common in the county.

In more recent times, Wexford was the focus of the rebellion of 1798. Inspired by ideals of the French Revolution, a group known as the United Irishmen staged their own revolution. It was a brave and wholehearted insurrection which ended after six weeks of constant fighting with a bloody battle on Vinegar Hill. Heroes such as Father John Murphy are remembered by memorials in towns throughout the county.

An outstanding area for birdwatching and a good place to see talented hurley players in action, Wexford has a feature peculiar to itself; here in the ancient baronies of Forth and Bargy in the southeast corner, you may still hear the old Saxon Yola dialect.

COURTOWN

Courtown, they say, has the least recorded rainfall anywhere in Ireland, which may explain why during the summer this popular holiday resort is action-packed and bursting with families – every house seems to offer accommodation and everywhere you look are caravans and mobile homes. The shops are stocked with souvenirs, the small, compact harbour is chock-a-block with pleasure boats and the sandy strand is a carpet of towels, parasols and pleasure-seekers.

For the passing traveller, the best time to visit is definitely out of season when the funfair has come to a weary halt and the holiday parks are deserted. Then is the time to fully appreciate the quiet beauty of this lovely harbour town on the River Ounavarra. Wrap up warm and there are plenty of invigorating walks along the coast with splendid views out to sea, or you can simply sit and watch the sea lashing against the rocks or the fishermen mending their nets beside the harbour.

BLACKWATER

Although tiny, this charming coastal village is well worth a stop – it must surely be one of the most picturesque spots in the county. Winner of several awards for tidiness and cleanliness, it is a photographer's dream. The village, which is situated as the name suggests on the gently flowing River Blackwater, has several surprises for the visitor: a miniature thatched cottage nestling down by the bridge; a few yards away an unusual shrine to Our Lady built around small waterfalls and decorated with shells; and opposite a house completely coated in shells.

WEXFORD WILDFOWL RESERVE,
North Slob, Wexford. Tel: (053) 23129

Flat, open and marshy, the Wexford Slobs were reclaimed from Wexford Harbour over 130 years ago. Migrating geese soon made this rather bleak, wind-blown spot their winter home, coming here to feed and rest on the Slobs by day, then roost in the harbour at night. Today, some 400 acres of the North Slob have been designated as a feeding and breeding ground for wildfowl. As maps and charts in the reception area indicate, the area offers very diverse habitats and attracts a wide variety of geese and wading birds.

Winter is the busiest time. In October and November visiting wildfowl arrive in flocks making a quite spectacular sight. Over 5,000 white-fronted geese – that's over half the world population – are regular lodgers. Others include pintails, Bewick's swans, black-tailed godwits and spotted redshanks. Rare birds such as the pink-footed goose have also been spotted on the Slobs. An observation tower (no binoculars are provided so take your own) gives panoramic views over the reserve, across the shallow, sandy estuary to the wooded conservation area at Raven Point, and out to Tern Island, named after the large colony of terns that descend on it in the summer months.

Open: all year, daylight hours
Admission free

WEXFORD
Tourist Information: Crescent Quay. Tel: (053) 23111

One of the most striking features of the county town of Wexford is its narrow streets. Indeed, they are so narrow that even in the main street there's a point where you can shake hands with someone on the opposite pavement. Wexford has a character all of its own, the winding streets and quaint shops giving it an intimate feel. The atmosphere is friendly and informal in this close-knit harbour town, which is so beautifully compact it is easy to find your way around alone. But for a colourful insight into the town's long history and

41

traditions, it's worth joining one of the regular guided tours led by members of the Old Wexford Society (details from the Tourist Office).

The Wexford area has been inhabited since at least 5000 BC. It was first marked on the map in the second century AD by the Roman geographer Ptolemy as Menapia, after a tribe who were thought to live in the area. Then came the Vikings who developed the town as a trading post. They named their settlement at the mouth of the River Slaney Waesfjord, 'the harbour of mud flats'. The town was taken by Cromwell in 1649 in a siege almost as bloody as the massacre of Drogheda (see page 214). The following century, Wexford was taken yet again, but this time only temporarily, by the insurgents of the 1798 rebellion. A bronze statue in the Bull Ring, once the scene of bull-baiting, was put up in 1905 to commemorate the rebellion.

The area around Wexford is dotted with attractions such as Johnstown Castle Gardens (see p. 43) and The Irish National Heritage Park (see p. 44), which can be easily reached by car or bicycle. However, there's a shortage of places of particular historic interest in the town itself with the exception of the remains of the twelfth-century Selskar Abbey which are well worth visiting. It was here in 1169 that the first treaty between the Irish and the Normans was signed. Three years later, Henry II of England did penance here for the murder of Thomas à Becket. Take note too of the statue of one of Wexford's most famous sons, John Barry, 'Father of the American Navy' (1745–1803). The bronze monument stands on Crescent Quay just outside the Tourist Office.

Above all, Wexford is famed for its opera festival held in October each year. The Wexford Opera Festival, founded in 1951, is grand opera on a grand scale – evening dress should most certainly be worn. It is a major festival of music and the arts, the whole town is taken over by opera-lovers intent on celebrating in style. What makes the festival so special is that it is a launching pad for new talent. Only amateurs perform and the works, although by masters, are rarely produced elsewhere.

Selskar Abbey, Westgate
Open: all the time
Admission free

Wexford Festival
For more information contact the
Tourist Office

JOHNSTOWN CASTLE GARDENS
and the IRISH AGRICULTURAL MUSEUM
Tel: (053) 42888

Romantic images spring to mind at the very first sight of this impressive Gothic-revival style mansion. Built around a thirteenth-century castle, it positively exudes all the drama and intrigue of a past age. Johnstown Castle was the ancestral home of the Esmonde family until they were dispossessed by Cromwell in 1649 and the estate sold by one of his soldiers to the Grogan family from England. Their descendants lived here until 1945 when the castle and its 1,000 acres were presented to the nation for use as an agricultural research centre.

The mansion itself is not, unfortunately, open to the public but you can at least get a glimpse of its splendour by calling into the entrance hall where there is visitor information on offer. You are also free to wander around the delightful grounds and picnic in the old sunken garden. The grounds have some fascinating scenic walks: through the ornamental gardens with over 200 different kinds of trees and shrubs; around the three ornamental lakes awash with wildfowl; past the hothouses and walled gardens; and to Rathlannon Castle, a ruin of a medieval tower house. Children can run wild, parents can gently stroll through these magnificent gardens.

Standing in the grounds, providing a sharp contrast to the grandeur of the castle, is the Irish Agricultural Museum, full of exhibits illustrating the tough way of life in rural Ireland through the centuries. The museum is appropriately housed in the old farmyard buildings of the Johnstown Castle estate – and thanks to the cattle kept in nearby fields there's an authentic smell to greet you! The rooms are superbly laid out with a large but manageable selection of all the weird and wonderful tools and machinery used on the farm and by country craftsmen. There are displays on rural transport, farming and farmyard activities, including a dairy and a complete country kitchen; reconstructed craft workshops; old photographs; an important collection of Irish country furniture and more.

Castle Grounds
Open: daily, 9.00–17.30
Admission charge

Agricultural Museum
Open: June–Aug, Mon–Fri,
9.00–17.00; Sat and Sun,
14.00–17.00; May and Sept–Oct,
Mon–Fri, 9.00–12.30, 13.30–17.00;
Sat and Sun, 14.00–17.00; Nov–Apr,
Mon–Fri, 9.00–12.30, 13.30–17.00
Admission charge

THE IRISH NATIONAL
HERITAGE PARK
Ferrycarrig, Wexford. Tel: (053) 41733 or 23111

A history lesson at a glance, this open-air museum aims to guide the visitor through 9,000 years of Ireland's heritage showing life through the centuries from the Stone Age to medieval times. The 33-acre park, on the site of an important fort built by the Norman Robert Fitz-stephen after he captured Wexford in 1169, is dotted with full-scale replicas of homes and settlements from the Mesolithic camp site of the country's earliest inhabitants to Norman motte and bailey. There's a ring fort and souterrain, an early Christian monastic site, a crannog (man-made island), a Viking ship, a horizontal mill, a round tower and much more. Information plaques at each site give a full explanation.

It is an ambitious and on-going project criticized by some as being 'plastic history on a plate'. But for anyone wanting a quick introduction to Irish history in a two-hour session it's all here. Although the models are not authentic, with the help of experts in the field they are as far as possible exact copies of the originals found in different parts of Ireland. Materials have been chosen to give a true picture and the method of construction carefully planned – you won't find any six-inch nails here! The varied landscape of the park (a nature trail leaflet is available from the reception area) has meant that each reconstruction can be slotted into an appropriate environment. Eventually it is hoped to complete the story by planting the trees and flowers that would have grown at the relevant times.

Open: Mar–end Oct, daily,
09.00–19.00

Admission charge

LADY'S ISLAND

If you're planning to explore the scenic area between Rosslare Harbour and Carnsore Point, you'll need a map. The winding roads seem to wind in all the wrong directions. It is worth persevering, though: Lady's Island is a lovely spot. Lying just south of Carnsore Point, it is in an almost completely enclosed sea inlet and linked by a causeway to the mainland. Named Lady's Island after the ancient monastery dedicated to the Blessed Virgin that once stood here, it has long been a place of pilgrimage. Penitent pilgrims still come to the island annually on 15 August.

Of interest on the island, a popular birdwatching site, are the ruins of an Augustinian priory and a twelfth-century Norman castle, known for its leaning tower. Six miles out to sea is the Tuskar Rock, guarded by a flashing light that can be seen 30 kilometres distant. As you travel westwards from Lady's Island to Kilmore Quay look out for the signs to the Tacumshane Windmill. This much-photographed mill has been beautifully preserved with whitewashed walls and a thatched roof.

Priory and Castle
Open: daylight hours
Admission free

Tacumshane Windmill
Open: daylight hours
Admission free

KILMORE QUAY

The county of Wexford is noted for its thatch, and the small fishing village of Kilmore Quay is the place to come to admire local craftsmanship. Cottage after cottage is topped with a trim thatch giving the village a charming picture-postcard appearance. But the thatched cottages are far from the only attraction of this lovely spot. Kilmore Quay is known for its good fishing, its waters are abundant with mackerel, sole, gurnard, ray and flatfish. It is also a leaving point for boats taking birdwatchers to the Saltee Islands, Ireland's largest bird sanctuary. The two uninhabited islands have become a breeding ground for seabirds, especially gannets, cormorants, shags and kittiwakes.

For a good view of the village, out to the Saltee Islands and eastwards along the flat coast, board Kilmore Quay's latest addition, the lightship *Guillemot*, and climb carefully up the steep stairway to the Bridge Deck. *Guillemot* was built in 1922 and saw continuous service around the Irish coast until the late 1960s. She was converted into a maritime museum and berthed at Wexford Quay but, after much vandalism, was put up for sale. The enterprising members of the Kilmore Quay Maritime Society bought the *Guillemot* and began a major restoration project. Eventually they plan to have everything completely shipshape, a true reflection of life aboard, with every piece of original furniture polished and every instrument in working order. It is an on-going project but at the time of writing was well underway and there was already much to interest the maritime-minded visitor.

Museum   **Admission charge**
Open: St Patrick's weekend
(Fri–Sun), 14.00–17.00; Easter
weekend (Sat–Mon), 14.00–17.00;
May, Sat and Sun, 14.00–17.00;
June–Sept, Mon–Fri, 14.00–20.00;
Sat and Sun, 12.00–18.00

HOOK HEAD

The best time to visit Hook Head is on a stormy day when the waves lash dramatically against the rocks and the sea is a wash of white splash. Wild and windswept, it's a gloriously remote spot at the very tip of County Wexford. The attractive lighthouse here is probably the oldest in Europe. Built in the twelfth century on the site of an earlier beacon, it is the proud boast of locals that a light has been kept almost continuously for 1,500 years. Look across the sea and you can also spot the lighthouse at Dunmore East (see page 57).

With the sea air blowing in strong gusts, Hook Head is the perfect place for a bracing walk. Follow the rugged coastline and enjoy the views out over the Waterford Estuary to Waterford City (see page 54) or clamber along the limestone rocks, which are surprisingly rich in fossils. Don't be surprised to see scuba divers plunging into the water around Hook Head; excellent underwater visibility makes it a popular scuba-diving centre.

The craggy Hook peninsula itself, which is only 4 m across at its widest point and ½ m at its narrowest, can be explored by following the 48 km Ring of Hook drive, which takes in the villages and attractions of note along the way. Included in the tour is the beach at Baginbun, the landing place of the Norman invaders in 1170, where as the old rhyme goes: 'At the creake of Baginbun, Ireland was lost and won.'

Hook Tower   **Admission free**
Open: exterior, all the time

BALLYHACK

For most visitors the only reason to visit this small village is to catch the ferry across to Passage East (see p. 54). While you wait, however, there is much to please the eye, and if you feel like indulging yourself the Neptune Restaurant (Tel: (051) 89284) has a mouth-watering menu with sea food a speciality. The busy harbour coloured by fishing boats is overlooked by the ruins of five-storey sixteenth-century Ballyhack Castle, once owned by the Knights Templar, and offers lovely views of Passage East and Waterford Harbour. The ferry is the short cut into County Waterford. You may, however, prefer to travel via the road which skirts the estuary of the River Barrow, taking you past Dunbrody Abbey (see page 48) and the John F. Kennedy Park (see page 48) to New Ross, an ancient town founded by Isobel, the daughter of Strongbow, and now a major inland port.

The River Barrow rises in the Slieve Bloom mountains in County Laois, then meanders its way across country to flow into the sea here at Waterford Harbour. A fun way to enjoy the river is to take a trip on one of the Galley Cruising Restaurants (Tel: (051) 21723 for details), which leave daily from New Ross during the summer months. Lunch, afternoon tea or dinner is served aboard, and is of surprisingly good quality.

DUNBRODY ABBEY
Nr Campile

A visit to Dunbrody, 'the noblest pile in Ireland', is inspiring – you can't help but wonder why these majestic twelfth-century monastic ruins beside the winding River Barrow are still so undiscovered. Just be grateful that they are! The large Cistercian abbey was built by the monks of St Mary's Abbey in Dublin in around 1190. Well protected by royal enactments, it became an important house with the abbot enjoying a powerful and influential position in his domain. The last abbot, Alexander Devereaux, surrendered to the Crown in 1536 and was made the first bishop of the nearby town of Ferns. The abbey ruins are in remarkably good condition. Of particular note is the richly ornamented West Door and also the fine lancet windows.

Open: all the time
(key from caretaker nearby)
Admission free

THE JOHN F. KENNEDY PARK
Nr Campile. Tel: (051) 88171

John F. Kennedy, President of the USA (1961–3) had, like so many eminent Americans, Irish roots. His great-grandfather was born in Dunganstown near New Ross in a cottage still lived in by descendants of the family. Jack Kennedy left for America in 1848, fleeing from the famine, to start a new life. This park, close to Dunganstown, a memorial and tribute to his famous great-grandson, was built following John F. Kennedy's assassination and funded by United States citizens of Irish origin.

Nestling in the southern slopes of Slieve Coillte (Hill of the Forest), the park is vast. The centrepiece is the internationally renowned Arboretum, which has over 4,500 types of trees and shrubs (all neatly labelled), mostly given as presents from all over the world. The rest of the 600-acre park is equally attractive with pockets of interest in all corners and some delightful places to stop for a picnic. Unless you plan to travel by one of the pony and traps that tour the park in the summer months, be prepared for a long walk. To find out the best routes to follow, call into the visitor centre and ask about signposted walks.

The highest point of the park, some 266 m above sea level and reached by a road up the heather-covered mountainside, has panoramic views over Carlow and Wexford to the south and the counties of Waterford and Kilkenny to the east.

Open: May–Aug, daily, 10.00–20.00; Apr and Sept, daily, 10.00–18.30; Oct–Mar, daily, 10.00–17.00

Admission charge (car park only)

COUNTY WATERFORD

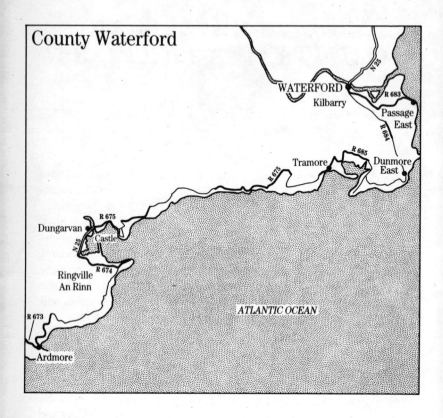

COUNTY WATERFORD

County Waterford teems with life in the summer. The long coastline, studded with sandy beaches washed by the warm Gulf Stream, with sheltered coves and popular holiday resorts, is a bustle of activity during the high season. But Waterford is a seaside county with a difference, for beyond the strands, high cliffs, amusement parks and maze of caravan parks the beauty of the gentle rolling countryside and wooded river valleys is an unexpected pleasure. A third dimension is added by the mountain ridges that frame the fertile land: the Comeragh range with its sparkling tarns, the Knockmealdowns and the Monavullagh Mountains with the spectacular Mahon Falls.

The county, famed for its fine crystalware, is neatly circumscribed by rivers to the north and west, and the Atlantic sea to the south. The River Suir flows through the broad plains of Tipperary eastwards through Clonmel and then opens into the estuary of Waterford Harbour. To the west is the River Blackwater, known for its coarse fishing, which rises in County Kerry, continues east through Cork and then turns southwards to flow into Youghal Bay. This river, named 'The Irish Rhine' because of its everchanging riverside scenery, is at its most beautiful in County Waterford where it passes through the pretty and historic villages of Lismore and Cappoquin.

The area around Dungarvan, now the administrative centre for the county, is often called Deise country. This name comes from the Deise tribe who settled here in the third century and had a strong influence on the whole county. Deep in the heart of Deise country is the Gaeltacht of An Rinn, a thriving centre of Irish Gaelic language and culture, unique to the southeast coast of Ireland.

The car ferry which runs a continuous service across the Suir estuary between Ballyhack and Passage East saves a great deal of time, cutting the journey between Wexford and Waterford by around an hour. The five-minute crossing also offers some of the best views of Passage East, a pretty village at the foot of a steep hill. Three km north and worth visiting is the splendid viewpoint at the top of Cheekpoint Hill. Just south of Passage East on the road to Dunmore East (see page 57) are a few sparse remains of the Geneva Barracks, one-time prison for the rebels of the 1798 uprising. Why Geneva? Well, the barracks were originally built in 1785 as a home and workspace for goldsmiths and silversmiths from Geneva. However, the project didn't materialize and the barracks were used first by British soldiers and then later as a prison. The ruins, marked by a plaque, have been made famous by the much-sung ballad 'The Croppy Boy' (crop-headed United Irishman), which commemorates the part the barracks played in the 1798 rebellion:

> At Geneva Barracks the young man died
> And at Passage they have his body laid
> Good people who live in peace and joy
> Give a prayer and a tear for the Croppy Boy.

Geneva Barracks   **Open:** all the time
                                       Admission free

WATERFORD
Tourist Information: 41, The Quay. Tel: (051) 75788

Strategically placed on the River Suir, the county town of Waterford was once an important Viking settlement. Fortifications dating back to the Viking occupation in the ninth century still dot the old part of the city adding to the charm of the narrow streets and Georgian buildings. Indeed, Waterford is said to have more ancient walls than any other Irish city with the exception of Derry (see page 168). Most impressive of the remains is **Reginald's Tower**, a circular tower and the only surviving bastion of Viking power in Ireland. Built in 1003, it is named after Reginald MacIvor, a Dane by origin and Governor of Waterford at the time. Over the years it has been used as a fortress, prison, military stores depot, a mint and an air-raid shelter. It is now home for the city museum with exhibitions and displays tracing the history and development of Waterford.

Waterford is essentially an industrial city, its growth based on the food and engineering industries. As with most industrial cities, first impressions are not always good. A walk around the city will soon change your mind, however. And if you want to be sure to cram in all the sights there's a signposted walking trail available from Reginald's Tower. Close to the tower is **St Olaf's Church**, founded in around 870 AD and dedicated to the Vikings' favourite saint. The church was rebuilt and restored over the years, and only a small fragment of the original building now remains. Other notable monuments in the area are the roofless but extensive ruins of the splendid '**French Church**' (or Grey Friars), a Franciscan monastery founded in 1240 which survived the suppression to become a hospice and later a Huguenot chapel; **Christchurch Cathedral**, built on the site of the original eleventh-century cathedral, and **Holy Trinity Cathedral** with its richly decorated interior.

Two eighteenth-century buildings worth visiting are the **Waterford Chamber of Commerce** in George's Street with its magnificent oval staircase and decorative stucco work by a local artist, and the **City Hall** in the Mall. Here in the Council Chamber is a glorious cut-glass chandelier, made by the craftsmen in the local Waterford Glass factory (see page 56). A complete and priceless old Waterford crystal dinner service is also on display. The city is world famous for its distinctive glassware.

The **Theatre Royal** in the Mall is the only surviving rotunda-type Victorian theatre in Ireland. It stages regular productions by local and visiting companies and is host to the International Festival of Light Opera held in late September each year.

Reginald's Tower. Tel: contact Tourist Information
Open: May–Sept, Mon–Fri, 11.00–13.00, 14.00–19.00; Sat, 11.00–14.00
Admission charge

St Olaf's Church
Open: reasonable hours
Admission free

The French Church
Open: reasonable hours
Admission free

Christchurch Cathedral
Open: reasonable hours
Admission free

Holy Trinity Cathedral
Open: reasonable hours
Admission free

Waterford Chamber of Commerce
Tel: (051) 72639
Open: all year, Mon–Fri, office hours
Admission free

City Hall. Tel: (051) 73501
Open: by arrangement
Admission free

Theatre Royal. Tel: (051) 74402
Open: telephone for performance details

WATERFORD CRYSTAL
Kilbarry (3 km west of Waterford on the Cork Road)
Tel: (051) 73311

It's an experience just to wander around the gallery and soak up the glittering elegance of the famous Waterford crystalware from the daintiest of liqueur glasses and napkin rings to the shimmering chandeliers and centrepieces. However, visitors can also see behind the scenes of the factory, the largest of its kind in the world. There are regular guided tours or alternatively you can watch a continuous video explaining the manufacturing process.

On the tour the guide explains how the story of Waterford Crystal began back in 1783 when the first factory was opened. Now, as then, each piece is made by hand. The craftspeople still work with the type of tools and methods that have been used for hundreds of years. It's a highly skilled craft requiring a great deal of precision and concentration. First, a mixture of materials is placed in an oil-fired furnace and heated to an incredible 1,200°C to form molten glass. The blower then takes over and blows the molten glass into a smooth crystal shape. Finally comes the exquisite cutting and engraving, a time-consuming task which calls for talent, dedication and plenty of patience.

The tour ends, as you might expect, with an invitation to buy some famous Waterford Crystal, but perfection is the motto at Waterford and there are no seconds so don't expect any bargains.

Open: Mon–Fri, 09.00–17.00.   **Admission free**
Tours from 10.15 to 14.30. Book in
advance.

DUNMORE EAST

The coast road from Passage East to Tramore takes you past some lovely sandy beaches and busy fishing harbours. Dunmore East, set against a backdrop of high cliffs coloured with sea pinks, makes a particularly pretty stopping place. It's so like a picture postcard with lighthouse and gaily painted thatched cottages, it's hard to believe you're not standing in a film set. Indeed, Maeve Binchy's book *Echoes* was actually filmed here in 1988.

However, this seaside resort with its sheltered beach and excellent waters for surfing and boardsailing is, in fact, a major centre for sea angling both for business and pleasure. A large fishing fleet is based at the harbour, bringing in catches of such delicacies as lobster and crayfish, available fresh at very reasonable prices. The harbour itself was designed in 1814 to cater for Dunmore's growth as a centre for the herring industry. It was also a station for mail boats travelling between England and the south of Ireland.

Just a few miles away on the west side of Waterford Harbour is a village called Crooke which looks out over the Suir estuary to Hook Head (see page 46). You will probably have heard of the saying 'by hook or by crook'; well, it was from these two places that the famous phrase originated. When Cromwell was planning to take Waterford he had to decide whether to arrive by Hook or by Crooke.

Tramore is one of Ireland's most popular seaside resorts. With its three-mile beach and wealth of amenities, it acts like a magnet for families in search of sun, sea, safe bathing and plenty of entertainment. It is best avoided in the height of the summer when the 50-acre amusement park, pier, brightly coloured cafés and beach are completely taken over by holidaymakers. Out of season, you can enjoy bracing strolls amid the splendid scenery of the area.

With Tramore as a starting point, there are plenty of choices for invigorating walks. For a fairly leisurely excursion, follow the promenade and beach to the Burrows, a series of sandhills just east of the town. Or head for Kilbride with its ruins of a church, old castle and earthworks, then continue along the campion-covered route to the Knockdeen Dolmen. A longer trek offering some beautiful views is provided by the Doneraile footpath over the Doneraile Cliffs and on to the Great Newtown Head. Here, at the end of the walk, on the precarious cliff edge, are three white pillars, one of which supports the Metal Man, an iron figure of a soldier pointing out to sea. Tradition has it that any young girl who hops around the base of the pillar on one foot will soon be married.

The coast road from Tramore to Dungarvan is dotted with lovely villages and sandy beaches – if time allows, attractive places to spend some time are Annestown, Bunmahon, Stadbally and Clonea.

DUNGARVAN

Dungarvan, a busy port and market town on the River Colligan, dates far back in history to the Stone Age. Hidden in the name Dungarvan is the clue to the town's later history. Originally named after the monastic settlement founded here in the seventh century by St Garvan, the word Dun, which means fortress, was added after a castle was built on the harbour's edge. Dungarvan Castle with its imposing circular keep was built by King John in 1185 but was much altered over the years and then finally destroyed by Cromwell in 1649. You're free to wander around the remains and to follow the remnants of the old town walls, but these are rather unimpressive unless you're acquainted with their history.

So, to find out more, call in for a drink at one of the nearby pubs. You'll probably be told about the canny woman who is said to have saved the town from Cromwell's army by drinking the health of the Lord Protector at the town gates. Ask too about the legendary greyhound, Master McGrath, who was defeated only once in thirty-seven races. There's a monument to him at Ballymacmague, just a few miles away. However, you're unlikely to find any explanation for the curious gable-like structure in the churchyard known as the Holed Gable. Its origin has defeated experts for many years.

Today, Dungarvan has a special attraction for fishing enthusiasts – boats leave regularly from the harbour in search of shark and other deep-sea fish. It is also the gateway to the mountainous area of West Waterford. To the north are the peaceful Comeraghs and Monavullaghs, and to the west the Knockmealdown Mountains. Although off the coast road, if you have time make a detour through the mountains by following one of three truly beautiful drives; the circular Comeragh Drive with continuously changing mountain scenery, the Nore Valley Drive with its wooded glens and tumbling streams, or the 'Vee' road through the Knockmealdown range. All have plenty of stopping points for walks and picnics.

Dungarvan Castle
Open: all the time
Admission free

AN RINN

Just south of Dungarvan is the peninsula of An Rinn, or Ring, where the Irish language and culture still thrives. The peninsula boasts some superb coastal views, especially from the harbour at Helvick Head, and the winding roads make for interesting exploration – although if you find yourself getting lost, you won't be the only one. Signposting, which is in Irish Gaelic, is rather haphazard but thankfully the locals are most friendly and will point you in the right direction.

In the village of Ring itself, there's an Irish language college which holds popular summer courses and organizes a variety of cultural activities such as evenings of traditional music, song, dance and folklore, to which everyone is invited. A mile from Ring is Bally-nagaul, a charming olde-worlde village where the people are proud to have Irish Gaelic as their first language and are happy to treat visitors to a smattering of their native tongue tinged with the broad Waterford accent.

An Rinn College
For further details of entertainment
and summer Irish Language
Courses contact: the Principal, Ring
College, Ring, County Waterford

ARDMORE MONASTIC RUINS
Ardmore

For peace and tranquillity visit the small seaside resort of Ardmore where the Irish novelist Molly Keane wrote *Good Behaviour* and *Time After Time*. The major point of interest at Ardmore is the graceful monastic ruins which stand on the site of the seventh-century settle-ment founded by St Declan, a missionary bishop who made his pilgrimage here even before St Patrick began to convert the Irish to Christianity. It's interesting to note from the names on the gravestones that Declan has long been the most popular first name in this area.

The main group of remains comprise St Declan's Oratory, a small early church reputed to be his grave and still a place of pilgrimage; the Round Tower, which stands 29 m high and is as perfect an example as you're likely to come across in Ireland; and the twelfth-century cathedral with magnificent figure carvings and Romanesque arching on the west gable. To help you appreciate the ruins there are infor-mative plaques explaining the main features of interest. If you find that the story of St Declan has captured your imagination then nearby are Temple Disert, and St Declan's Holy Well with its stone chair, three early stone crosses and a bathing vessel where pilgrims could wash. At the end of the sandy beach is St Declan's Stone, a huge glacial boulder, which he is believed to have used to transport his bell and vestments over the sea from Wales.

Open: all the time
Admission free

COUNTY CORK

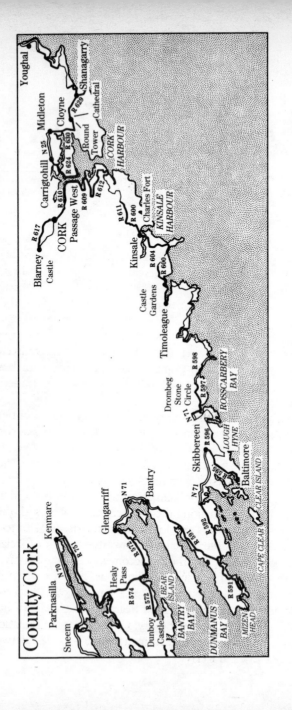

COUNTY CORK

Ireland's largest county, Cork, with its changing scenery and rich history, is often said to paint a picture of the country in miniature. And it's true – travelling from the fertile farmlands of the east to the wild and mountainous west, the scenery seems to change by the hour. You pass by isolated beaches, rocky headlands, secluded bays, busy fishing villages, dark forests and attractive river valleys that run between red sandstone ridges. And, of course, there are the lively pubs where locals are happy to point you in the direction of both the ancient monuments that dot the landscape and the latest attractions of the present.

The east and west of the county have quite separate identities; East Cork is dominated by the ancient city of Cork, now a major commercial centre with a busy harbour and international airport, West Cork is rugged and remote with an unspoilt beauty all of its own. The West Cork coast road stretches from the colourful sailing centre of Kinsale to the old mining town of Allihies on the western tip of the Beara Peninsula. It takes you along the southern coastline, much indented with island-studded bays and long sandy strands, and out to Mizen Head, which marks the extreme southwesterly point of Ireland. As you approach Bantry Bay the air becomes noticeably balmy. Here, warmed by the Gulf Stream, the climate is so moist and mild that succulent plants flourish in sub-tropical gardens. By sharp contrast, the Caha Mountains on the jagged Beara Peninsula appear bare and deserted and have an austere beauty. Crossed by the dramatic Healy Pass, this rocky mountain ridge forms a natural boundary between the counties of Cork and Kerry.

Youghal, pronounced 'yawl', is a town full of character and a favourite seaside resort for holidaymakers looking for safe, sandy beaches. With plenty of shops (including excellent fresh fish stalls), restaurants, a pleasant park and many other amenities, it makes an ideal stopping point to stock up on provisions. But don't count on a quick visit, there's so much of interest you'll soon find yourself wanting to know more about this historic town at the mouth of the Blackwater River with its well-preserved old town walls and towers. Perhaps the best way to discover the main features and antiquities is by following the Tourist Trail, a signposted walking tour which takes around an hour to complete.

Among the places of special interest is the impressive St Mary's Collegiate Church, a beautiful and awesome building. Inside is a richly carved monument to Richard Boyle, first Earl of Cork. Another notable character identified with Youghal is Sir Walter Raleigh, who was once the mayor. His house, Myrtle Court (not open to the public), is a fine but much altered Elizabethan building. Apparently it was in the garden of this house that he smoked the first tobacco and grew the first potatoes in Ireland. Mention should also be made of the Water Gate, sometimes known as 'Cromwell's Gate' because he is said to have passed beneath it when he sailed from Ireland in 1649.

STEPHEN PEARCE POTTERY
Shanagarry. Tel: (021) 646807

Overlooking Ballycotton Bay is Shanagarry where William Penn, founder of Pennsylvania, lived in 1667. The village is better known today for its pottery; leading Irish potter Stephen Pearce has set up a studio and opened the doors to the public. Pearce has become well known for his simple, functional yet elegant pottery: his earthenware with distinctive white glaze is popular all over Ireland. Although one pottery studio is much the same as another, visitors are made especially welcome here and the craftsmen are happy to tell you how Stephen learnt the art of pottery from his father. They will explain how local clay is dug for the pottery and peat cut for firing the kiln, and take you through the eighteen different hand processes involved. The idea, obviously, is that you'll make a purchase and the showroom is well stocked with the complete range. There's no obligation to buy but if simply designed and decorated handcrafted pottery is to your taste then you may find some of these pieces hard to resist.

Open: all year, Mon–Fri,   **Admission free**
08.00–17.00; Sat, 10.00–17.00; Sun,
14.00–17.00

CLOYNE CATHEDRAL AND ROUND TOWER
Cloyne

It's not often you get the opportunity to climb a round tower, but visitors are welcome to explore the ivy-clad tower which dominates the high street of the small village of Cloyne. It's a pretty precarious and very dimly lit ascent, but for the sure-footed it's quite an experience. The tower was originally 28 m high but was struck by lightning in 1749 and the conical top was destroyed. It was later replaced by battlements. The winding stairs take you right to the bell at the top with splendid views in all directions.

The cathedral is on the opposite side of the road. It was first built in around 1250 on the site of a monastery founded by St Colman, patron saint of Cloyne, in the sixth century. Although little of the early church remains there are many items of historic interest, including the monument to the great philosopher Bishop Berkeley (1685–1753), who was Bishop of Cloyne from 1734 to 1752. Children are always intrigued by the horseshoe carved in stone on the floor near the font. Many local children believe this is the devil's footprint but it's simply the sign of the Smyth family who lived in the area for many years.

Open: any reasonable time   **Admission charge**
(key obtainable from Cathedral
Cottage)

FOTA WILDLIFE PARK
Fota Island, Carrigtohill. Tel: (021) 812678/812736

Only ten miles from the centre of Cork City, the tranquil island of Fota can easily be reached by car and certainly shouldn't be missed. It's worth setting aside at least half a day to enjoy the Wildlife Park and the neighbouring attractions of Fota House and Fota Arboretum.

The wildlife park set in open, natural surroundings with charming wooded walks was created by the Royal Zoological Society of Ireland. The aim, which is being successfully achieved, is to provide a home and breeding ground for selected groups of endangered species such as cheetah and oryx. There are plenty of other animals here too, including kangaroos, ostriches, antelopes, monkeys, gibbons, emus, penguins, giraffes, zebras, flamingos and many more. The park, which covers around 80 acres, is thoughtfully designed so the animals have lots of space to roam as they wish. Visitors can walk amongst them, guided by paths with barriers that are so well concealed you can sometimes be in for a bit of a fright! Information plaques give details not only of the different animals but also the nearby trees and shrubs.

Fota House is a fine example of Regency architecture. Well restored and refurbished in period style, the main point of interest is the important collection of Irish landscape paintings, which date from the 1750s to the 1870s. The mild climate on Fota Island has helped many tender tree species to flourish and the Arboretum is now considered as possibly the finest in Ireland.

Fota Wildlife Park
Open: 1st Sat Apr–end Oct, daily, 10.00–17.15 (closes 18.00); Sun, 11.00–17.15 (closes 18.00)
Admission charge

Fota House Tel: (021) 812555
Open: 1st Sat Apr–end Oct, Mon–Sat, 11.00–18.00; Sun, 14.00–18.00. Rest of year: Sun and Bank Hols, 14.00–18.00
Admission charge

Fota Arboretum
Open: 1st Sat Apr–end Oct, daily, 10.00–17.15 (closes 18.00); Sun, 11.00–17.15 (closes 18.00)
Admission free

Cork City, 'The Venice of Ireland', with its waters crossed by hump-back bridges and stone staircases running down to quays and tree-lined walks, has a definite continental flavour. Its focal point is the much-loved River Lee, the subject of so many of the ballads still sung in the pubs of Cork. The 'lovely Lee' divides into two channels at the western side of the city, converges and widens at Custom House and then eventually flows into Cork Harbour. The heart of the city lies on the flat island between the two streams while to the north and south rise steep hills with narrow, crowded lanes evoking a quaint, olde-worlde atmosphere.

Cork, long known as a Festival City, plays host to a number of important cultural events during the year, including the Cork Film International Festival in September, the Cork International Choral and Folk Dance Festival in April or May and the Cork Jazz International Festival in October. Although the third largest city in Ireland, Cork is remarkably compact and is best explored on foot. A signposted Tourist Trail (booklet available from the Tourist Information Office) is a good way of making sure you don't miss the main sites.

Cork City Museum, Fitzgerald's Park, Mardyke. Tel: (021) 270679. This the place to go for an introduction to the city, past and present. The museum, set in the lovely Fitzgerald Park, a mile from the centre, has permanent displays and changing exhibitions which trace the city's history from around 600 AD when St Finbarre, the Fair Headed, founded a church and school on the south bank of the Lee. At the time of St Finbarre the whole area was a large swamp. Indeed, the name Cork is derived from the word Corcaigh, which means marshy place.

Open: all year, Mon–Fri, 11.00–13.00, 14.15–17.00; Sun 15.00–17.00; Closed Sat

Admission charge on Sun only

Patrick Street Another well-known landmark is the statue to Father Matthew, who was known as the Apostle of Temperance, in Patrick

Street. This street is one of the city's main shopping parades and is considered by Corkonians as 'the finest street in Ireland, if it wasn't for the bend'. Its strange curve is testament to the fact that Patrick Street, like Grand Parade and South Mall, were once waterways and still follow the course of ancient rivers.

Shandon Church and Tower, Shandon Street. Tel: (021) 501672. One of the most famous buildings in Cork must surely be Shandon Church with its giant pepperpot steeple. From the top of the tall tower (two sides are red limestone and the other two grey limestone) there are panoramic views of the city. However, for most visitors the main attraction is the eight bells about which 'Father Prout' (Sylvester O'Mahony) wrote the song 'The Bells of Shandon'.

Open: Mon–Sat, 10.00–16.00
(winter), 10.30–17.00 (summer)
Admission free

St Finbarre's Cathedral, Dean Street. Tel: (021) 964740. Standing on the site of St Finbarre's church is the French Gothic-style Cathedral of St Finbarre, described by Sir John Betjeman as 'a gem of a cathedral'. Huge and highly decorated, the cathedral has among its treasures a brass memorial to Elizabeth Aldworth, the only woman Freemason.

Open: Mon–Fri, 10.00–13.00,
14.00–17.30
Admission free

University College The city which flourished around the school founded by St Finbarre continues its tradition as a seat of learning with a thriving university whose motto is 'where Finbarre taught, let Munster learn'. University College has some fine collections of varied treasures, including rare books and stones carved in the ancient ogham alphabet. The little Honan Collegiate Chapel is of particular note. Built in Irish Romanesque style, it has some impressive stained glass windows.

Open: campus all year until 22.30;
building on request only
Admission free

BLARNEY CASTLE
Blarney. Tel: (021) 385278

Five miles inland from Cork, Blarney takes you a little way from the coastal route but if you're intrigued by the famous Blarney Stone then make for Blarney Castle. Legend has it that this block of limestone has special powers of giving eloquence to anyone who kisses it and the stone has become so famous that the word 'blarney' is now part of the English language. It is used to describe pleasant talk, intended to deceive without causing offence. The stone is set in the castle wall beneath the battlements and so if you've set your heart on kissing it, you need to bend backwards (holding onto an iron railing) from the parapet walk.

Blarney has become a sort of mecca for visitors to Ireland with tourists queueing to see the sights, a sharp contrast to the wild and desolate coastline. However, if you don't mind the hustle and bustle then the magnificent fifteenth-century castle with its massive keep and secret caves is worth visiting. There are fine views from the top of the pleasant parkland around the little Blarney Lake, which has given rise to many an Irish folktale, with the wooded hills of Muskerry in the background. Nearby, Blarney Castle House, a refurbished Scottish baronial-type house, is also open to the public.

Blarney village was planned in the late eighteenth century as a linen and wool processing centre. In more recent years it has become a popular craft centre. The Blarney Woollen Mills, a complex of shops, restaurants and bars under one roof, sells a varied selection of sweaters, kilts, scarves, jewellery and many other Irish-made goods and gifts.

Blarney Castle
Open: Mon–Sat, May, 9.00–19.00; June and July, 9.00–20.30; Aug, 9.00–19.30; Sept, 9.00–18.30. Sun, 9.30–17.30 (last admission half an hour before closing time)
Admission charge

Blarney Castle House
Open: June–mid-Sept, Mon–Sat, 10.00–17.30
Admission charge

Blarney Woollen Mills
Open: all year, daily, 09.00–18.00 (closes 20.00 June, July and Aug)
Admission free

CHARLES FORT
Kinsale. Tel: (021) 772684

The best way to appreciate the rich history of recently restored Charles Fort on the outskirts of Kinsale is by a guided tour which leaves on the hour. Lasting around an hour, the tour gives you not only a real feel for this huge star-shaped fort but also a fascinating social history. Built in the 1680s, the fort was in continuous use until 1921 but was then left to decay until 1973 when it was declared a National Monument. An exhibition shows the work involved in the extensive programme of repair and conservation.

Set in a picturesque spot overlooking Kinsale Harbour, the fort is a lovely place for a picnic and quiet stroll. More romantic visitors will also enjoy the story of the ghost of the White Lady. According to legend, the daughter of the governor was walking the battlements with her fiancé on the eve of their wedding. She saw some white flowers growing on the rocks below and wanted them. A sentry volunteered to pick them if the bridegroom-to-be agreed to take his place on guard. Sadly, he fell asleep at his post and was discovered by the governor who, unaware of the disguise, shot him dead for such bad conduct. The bride was in such distress at the news she flung herself from the battlements.

Across Kinsale Harbour are the earlier remains of another great star-shaped fortress, James Fort, which was built in 1601.

Open: Guide/Information service: **Admission charge**
mid-Apr to mid-June, Tues–Sat,
10.00–17.00; Sun, 14.00–17.00;
mid-June to mid-Sept, 10.00–18.30,
rest of year, Mon–Fri, 08.00–16.30
(except public holidays)

KINSALE

Well established as a gourmet town, Kinsale certainly lives up to its culinary reputation with an appetizing selection of restaurant menus on offer. Gourmet weeks, held from time to time, are always a major attraction but throughout the year people travel from miles around to sample the delights of the Cottage Loft, the White House, Jim Edwards and other eating houses. And there are some wonderfully bracing walks in the area to help the digestion.

However, there's much more to Kinsale than the food. A pretty, olde-worlde town with a strong appeal for fishing, sailing and watersports enthusiasts, it is full of history. A signposted walking tour guides you along the narrow winding streets taking in the main sites, including the courthouse built in 1706, now a museum; the thirteenth-century church of St Multrose, still in use, with its fascinating gravestones; and Desmond Castle, built in the sixteenth century and known as the 'French Prison' because prisoners, as many as 600 at a time, were kept here during the Napoleonic Wars.

The Battle of Kinsale was one of the turning points of European history. A Spanish fleet sailed into the harbour and took over the town. Irish forces marched down from the north to join them but they could not hold out against the English forces who had gained a decisive victory by 2 January 1602. The battle took place just north of the town, and the battlefield is signposted.

Kinsale Museum   **Admission charge**
Open: June–Oct, daily,
10.30–16.30; off-season, Tel: (021)
772044

TIMOLEAGUE CASTLE GARDENS
Timoleague, Bandon. Tel: (023) 46116

At the head of a pretty inlet between Clonakilty and Courtmacsherry is the village of Timoleague. The village is dominated by the majestic ruin of an early fourteenth-century Franciscan abbey, dramatically situated on the shore of a creek and once famed for the Spanish wine that could be landed there with relative ease. However, just a few minutes' drive away and definitely worth visiting are the less well known Timoleague Castle Gardens laid out and maintained over the past 150 years by the Travers family. You'll probably see them hard at work in the gardens and they'll be pleased to stop for a chat. Guided tours can also be arranged.

Although little is left standing of the castle, built in 1214 and subject of many a legend, the gardens are a showcase of colour, a testament to the mild, moist climate of West Cork. One of the best times to visit is June when the palm trees bear scented cream-white panicles and you can pick your own soft fruit from the walled garden, but there's something to please the eye whenever you go; frost-tender shrubs, flowering trees and plants flourish throughout the opening season. The gardens are very compact so don't expect too much, they can easily be seen in an hour or less. To ensure value for the small entrance fee, however, there's a children's playground and plenty of picnic spots. Garden produce and rooted cuttings are also on sale.

Open: Easter weekend and mid-May to mid-Sept, daily, 12.00–1800, or by arrangement

Admission charge

DROMBEG STONE CIRCLE
Nr Rosscarbery

Signposted from the road which runs between Glandore and Rosscarbery, the stone circle is reached by a narrow footpath well decked with wild flowers. One of the finest of the stone circles in West Cork, it is dramatically situated on a rugged and windy ridge. There are seventeen standing stones in the circle dated at between 153 BC and 127 AD. Excavations several years ago revealed a cremated body in a half-broken urn carefully hidden under the soil in the centre of the circle.

A short walk to the west of the standing stones are two round huts and a cooking pit with a stone trough that could hold 338 litres of water. Stones were once heated in a fire and then thrown into the spring water in the trough. The water would then boil within about half an hour and keep hot for nearly three hours so meat could be cooked in it. This prehistoric cooking method has been re-enacted here at Drombeg in recent years, and it still works successfully.

Open: all the time
Admission free

LOUGH INE (or HYNE)

This secluded and mysterious lake, encircled by wooded hills, is not only a beautiful spot but also a nature reserve and an important centre for marine biological research. The lake is unusual in that it is joined to the sea by a channel so narrow that the tidal waters flush through in torrents bringing with them an assortment of sealife. Lough Ine is believed to provide a complete picture of coastal marine life and scientists use it as a natural laboratory for detailed study. Displays and information plaques detail the main features of the lonely and romantic lake that is so often forgotten by visitors.

There are some lovely walks around the lake and in the surrounding woodland. One of the best routes is to follow the path that leads high up through the forest to the hilltop from where there are some impressive seaward and coastal views.

Open: all the time
Admission free

BALTIMORE AND CAPE CLEAR ISLAND

A small and pleasant fishing port, popular with yachting and sailing enthusiasts, Baltimore (no connection to the American city although locals may tell you otherwise) has had a very tempestuous history. The ruined castle which stands on a rock overlooking the harbour is a reminder of such stormy events as the legendary raid in the seventeenth century when the village was attacked by Algerian pirates and many of its inhabitants shipped to North Africa as slaves. There are fine views from the headland: looking in a southwesterly direction there's Sherkin Island, close to the mainland, then Cape Clear Island and further out the famous Fastnet Rock, Ireland's most southerly point. Sherkin Island (motorboats leave from the harbour) has some sandy beaches and interesting coves and ruins but for a day out to remember, take the ferry to the larger island of Cape Clear where the Irish language and traditions still survive. It is the birthplace of St Ciaran, 'first born of the saints of Ireland', and you can still see the site of his church and the holy well. There's also a youth hostel, seabird observatory, ruined castle and lighthouse and many beautiful walks for the intrepid visitor willing to explore the rugged footpaths. Take your binoculars and from the cliffs you can look out to the island-studded, sparkling blue waters of Roaringwater Bay; to Schull, a small and picturesque village at the foot of Mount Gabriel and now an international centre for wind-surfers; and to Mizen Head, the scene of many a shipwreck, where the harsh sea lashes against the high cliffs with a vengeance.

BANTRY HOUSE
Bantry. Tel: (027) 50047

If you visit Bantry House at the weekend, you may well be greeted personally by the owner, whose family have lived here for over 250 years. The lovely part-Georgian house overlooking the beautiful Bantry Bay was opened to the public in 1945, the first in Ireland to welcome paying visitors, but the present owner admits there was very little to see when he took it over in 1978. Indeed, he even planned to sell up at one point. However, inspired by interest in his family history, he moved into the house with his wife and children and set about a programme of restoration and refurbishment.

Today the house, set in colourful Italian gardens, makes a fascinating and uplifting place to visit, an unexpected treasure trove of furniture and *objets d'art* collected from all over Europe. The dining room is the grandest room of all, dominated by the large painting, which hangs over the fireplace, of a scene in a fruit market, painted in part by Rubens. However, every room has its own special charm. The rose drawing room, for example, with a magnificent Waterford Crystal chandelier and the Aubusson Royal Tapestries, made as a wedding gift for Marie Antoinette, has a wonderful view over the bay, Whiddy Island and the Caha Mountains to the north. More recent additions include tearooms serving home-baked cakes and snacks and a well-stocked shop. And if you fancy enjoying a little luxury, the White family also provide bed, breakfast and evening meal.

Open: all year, daily, 09.00–18.00   **Admission charge**
(closes 20.00 summer)

GARINISH ISLAND (ILNACULLIN)
Glengarriff. Tel: (027) 63040/61311

Glengarriff, set amidst wild and rugged countryside cut by green and shady glens, is a popular tourist spot. The bright boards and ever-eager salespeople can be rather off-putting for anyone wanting to stay away from the well-trodden path, but with its creeks, islands and mountain valleys there are plenty of places to escape to. One place definitely worth visiting is Garinish Island, the loveliest of the small islets in Bantry Bay. Boat trips leave at regular intervals to take people to and from this beautiful island where the climate is so mild there's an amazing profusion of colour and variety in its gardens.

For naturalists, gardeners and photographers the island, which covers 36 acres, is a positive delight; it is no exaggeration to say that it's like walking onto a tropical paradise. The main garden is the formal Italian garden with its lily pond and vibrant shrubs and flowers. Nearby is a miniature Japanese garden and rockery. From here, there's a choice of shady walks through the semi-wild with surprises in store at every turn: breathtaking vistas, unusual sub-tropical plants, magnolias, camellias, rhododendrons and rare conifers, a mock Grecian temple and a Martello tower with splendid views.

Open: July and Aug, Mon–Sat, 09.30–18.30; Sun, 11.00–18.00; Apr, May, June and Sept, Mon–Sat, 10.00–18.30; Sun, 13.00–18.00; Mar and Oct, Mon–Sat, 10.00–16.30; Sun, 13.00–17.00. Last landings one hour before closing.

Admission charge

Boat trips' departure points are signposted from the main street.

HEALY PASS
R574

From Glengarriff the road skirts Bantry Bay and takes you below the Sugar Loaf mountain. Standing 575 m high, it can easily be explored but remember Irish weather can be very unpredictable so take sensible precautions. The road continues along the heather-covered southern side of the mountainous Beara Peninsula until it forks at Acrigole Bridge. If it's a bright, clear day (avoid the pass when it's misty or raining) and you've plenty of nerve, take the right-hand turn and, heart-in-mouth, make a diversion from the coastal road to the spectacular Healy Pass across the Caha Mountains and into County Kerry.

The narrow rock-strewn road makes its tortuous way up and up and still further up through the mountains until you reach the windy summit, some 330 m above sea level. Here, drivers and passengers, walkers and cyclists can catch their breath before making the dare-devil descent to the beautiful Killmakillogue Harbour. As you venture across the bare mountains it's tempting to imagine you're exploring undiscovered country but any such romantic illusions are quickly shattered by the gift shop and tearooms with coaches parked outside. However, this need not spoil your enjoyment; from the heights of the Healy Pass, many visitors stand gasping in heady admiration at the truly magnificent and far-reaching views of the mountain of Knockowen, the dark green Glanmore Lough, dotted with small islets, and northwards to the Kenmare River and Iveragh Mountains.

Open: all the time
Admission free

DUNBOY CASTLE
Off R572

A rugged but well-signposted driveway leads you through a mass of magnificent rhododendron bushes to the remains of Dunboy Castle. Set in such beautiful surroundings, it's worth visiting simply for the views of Bere Island and beyond and makes a very pleasant picnic spot. The castle was the stronghold of O'Sullivan Bere, who held out valiantly against the English forces in June 1602. It was finally destroyed after a few days' fighting but the garrison refused to surrender until all the walls were completely down. Indeed, their leader, McGeohegan, even tried to blow up the powder magazine but before he could get to it he fell dead from wounds, his torch in his hand.

Excavated and easily explored, the little that remains of the castle and star-shaped fort stands behind the burnt-out shell of the grand nineteenth-century mansion of the Puxey family. It is the story of this family, who made their fortunes from the copper mines at nearby Allihies, that provides the basis for Daphne du Maurier's novel *Hungry Hill*. You can see Hungry Hill itself (675 m) by looking northwards from Dunboy to the Slieve Miskish range of mountains.

Open: all the time
Admission free

COUNTY KERRY

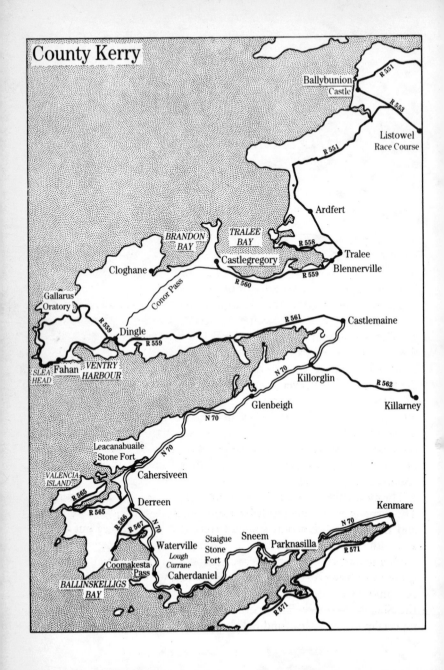

COUNTY KERRY

County Kerry, in the extreme southwest of Ireland, is a favourite haunt for painters, photographers and poets trying to capture some of its outstanding and contrasting scenery – the rocky mountains, gushing streams, sparkling lakes and bogs covered in native wild flowers such as St Patrick's cabbage and the greater butterworth. However, the weather in Kerry is notoriously unpredictable, changing from day to day, even hour to hour: strong winds blow up from the Atlantic, heavy rain and sea mists shroud the countryside. For visitors on a whistle-stop tour the dull weather can lead to disappointment but for those with time and patience it adds to the fascination of the county. For when the rain stops or the mist lifts the views are unexpectedly spectacular, the light bright, the colours vivid and the countryside glistening.

The mountainous area of South Kerry is most popular with visitors. The three large hilly peninsulas of Beara, Iveragh (the Ring of Kerry) and Dingle boast not only some of Ireland's finest scenery but also a wealth of well-preserved ancient monuments. Killarney, a little further inland, with its famous lakes, mountains and woods, attracts thousands of visitors each year. By contrast the terrain of North Kerry is an undulating lowland of moors and bogs stretching northwards to the Shannon estuary. The coast road has some lovely cliff scenery especially at Kerry Head and Ballybunion.

The Iveragh Peninsula, the largest of the peninsulas which stretch out into the Atlantic, is an area of outstanding beauty. The picturesque coast road which hugs the shoreline is known as the Ring of Kerry and is particularly scenic on a clear, bright day. Take a camera and several rolls of film; you'll want a record of the fine views and contrasting mountain and coastal scenery. A traditional starting point for a tour of the Ring of Kerry is from Killarney (see page 88), however you can also set off from Kenmare as described here. The route can be followed in a day, albeit a rather hurried one. If you're taking things at a more leisurely pace then there are plenty of stopping places and viewpoints along the way. A word of warning, though, as the peninsula is so mountainous there are few deviations from the main coastal road, and with many coaches and heavy tourist traffic in the summer, progress can be rather slow.

Taking **Kenmare** as your starting point, follow the N70 towards Waterville. Kenmare, a small seaside resort, is situated at the base of the long inlet known as the Kenmare River which separates the Beara and Iveragh peninsulas. Set in splendid scenery, the town has become a base for walkers and motorists but has much to offer the passing visitor. Historians will be keen to see the ancient monument known as the Druids' Circle, a fine stone circle on the banks of the River Finnihy. There are fifteen standing stones encircling a boulder burial made of three upright stones and a large capstone. It's hard to find so you may have to ask the way. Also well tucked away but worth searching out is St Clare's Convent, built in 1861 and renowned for its lace and embroidery. Sadly the art is now dying out, but knock on the door of the lace room and one of the nuns will show you their exquisite work.

As you leave Kenmare, to your right are the foothills of **Mac-Gillicuddy's Reeks**, red sandstone hills which rise above the lakes of Killarney. Among this range is Ireland's highest mountain, Carrantoohill, which towers to 1,041 m. The road takes you through pretty villages, beauty spots such as Parknasilla where exotic plants flourish in the mild climate, and past viewing points where you can admire the deep gorges, lush valleys and scattered lakes. Travel along the road through Sneem with its salmon weather vane, a sign of the good salmon fishing in the area, until you come to Castlecove and then follow the signs to **Staigue Fort**.

Although the sign indicates that the fort is only one and a half miles away, as the rough, undulating track winds its way through the lonely mountain valley, it feels more like ten. But keep going, the imposing ruins of this 2,000-year-old stone fortress are worth the trek. Standing in a field where sheep graze oblivious to its historical and archaeological importance, is the massive circular drystone Staigue Fort. The fort can be seen from the road but if you want to take a closer look then you must cross private land and may be asked for a small entrance fee. Exploring the interior you will find two little rooms in the walls and if you climb the perfectly formed stone steps to the platform on the inside wall, you'll be rewarded with yet more lovely views out to sea.

Just beyond the village of Westcove, you come to Caherdaniel. Nearby is **Derrynane House**, ancestral home of Daniel O'Connell (1775–1847), lawyer, politician and statesman, and one of the most influential figures in Irish history. This house, where he grew up and which in later years he used as a country home, is now a museum devoted to his life and career. With an assortment of relics, mementos, photographs and portraits, it's an important place to visit for anyone interested in the history of Ireland. It is rather dark and the layout lacks imagination but any dreariness is compensated for by the enthusiasm of the well-informed staff. They will take you around, point out specific items of interest and share intriguing stories about 'The Liberator'. There's also a 25-minute audio-visual presentation designed to give a greater insight into his aims and achievements.

If the house itself doesn't hold much attraction, then explore the 300-acre **Derrynane Park** with its pleasant walks through changing scenery and an exciting nature trail along the sand dunes. But parents, take care; it's an ideal haunt for 'hide and seek'. There's also a wildfowl sanctuary where dunlin, oystercatchers and other waders can often be seen. On Abbey Island, reached by foot across the sand, stand the ruins of Ahamore Abbey and the burial place of many of the O'Connells. Look out for a wild flower known as the Kerry Lily on the island; the Derrynane district is the only place it grows in Ireland.

The road now rises upwards and crosses the Pass of Coomakista Gap with yet more spectacular views and then descends into

Ballinskelligs Bay. Look to the right and you'll see the lovely Lough Currane, surrounded by early Christian remains. The next stop is **Waterville**, once the favourite holiday destination of Charlie Chaplin, which lies on a thin strip of land between Ballinskelligs Bay and Lough Currane. It is a popular tourist resort with a championship golf course, good fishing, a craft centre selling locally-made art and craft work and some excellent restaurants. If you decide to set aside two days to follow the Ring of Kerry then this is a good place to stay the night. Walkers will enjoy the cliff walks which take you as far as Inny Strand and past the small beach known as Falvey's Cove. Although unsafe for bathing, there are rock pools full of fascinating shells on the beach and many different types of seaweed, including the edible carrageen, which is gathered in April and May then dried and used in several traditional Irish dishes.

The main N70 road now travels northwards through Derreen to Cahersiveen, birthplace of Daniel O'Connell. If you've time, it's worth taking a couple of diversions. First to Ballinskelligs, an Irish Gaelic-speaking village with an Irish Gaelic college and a lovely 6 km strand. Ballinskelligs is one of the main departure points for boats to the famous **Skellig Islands**, a group of rocky islands 14 km out to sea. The boats, however, are unlicensed and trips cannot be guaranteed as rough seas often make landings impossible. There are, nevertheless, fine views of these remote islands, which are a haven for seabirds such as gannets, kittiwakes, petrels and guillemots. The Great Skellig, or Skellig Michael, has remarkably well-preserved remains of an early monastic settlement dating back to around 600 AD.

Another detour from the main road is to Portmagee, reputedly named after an eighteenth-century smuggler, and then across the bridge to **Valencia Island**. This barren, rocky island so rich in history and legend is worth visiting simply for its truly beautiful views especially from Knightstown and Bray Head. It also makes a lovely picnic spot. However if time is limited go straight to Cahersiveen. Here, from the bridge across the Valencia River there are good views over Valencia Harbour and the remains of the fifteenth-century Ballycarbery Castle. Nearby are the ruins of two stone ring forts, **Cahergeal** and **Leacanabuaile**. The latter, dated around ninth or tenth century AD, is one of the few such forts to be excavated and inside you can see three stone beehive houses, once lived in by poor farmers and their families.

The undulating road takes you through the valley of Kells and into the small seaside and fishing resort of Glenbeigh, then on through bogland to **Killorglin**, a market town situated above the River Laune, famed for salmon fishing and home to many graceful swans. Once a fishing village, Killorglin grew into a strategic military town, although little of the old castle now remains. One relic of the past does still survive, however: the Puck Fair. Thousands of visitors flock to Killorglin for this traditional horse and cattle fair held from Thursday to Saturday during the second week of August. The centrepiece of the fair is a wild billy goat, or puck, which is brought from the mountains. Decorated with ribbons, he stands on a platform in the centre of the town and watches over proceedings. The origin of the fair is still the talking point in many local bars; no one has an answer although many believe it to be a form of ancient pagan fertility rite.

From Killorglin, you have two choices. If you intend to stick fairly closely to the coast road then continue along the N70 to Castlemaine, starting point for a tour of the Dingle Peninsula (see p. 90). Alternatively, head inland and spend a day in Killarney (see p. 88) and, if time permits, complete the full Ring of Kerry by driving over the scenic Moll's Gap and then back to Kenmare.

St Clare's Convent, Kenmare
Open: Lace Room: all year, daily except Sun and Holy Days,
10.30–12.00, 14.00–17.00
Admission free

Staigue Fort, Castlecove
Open: all the time
Admission free

Derrynane House, Caherdaniel
Tel: (0667) 5113
Open: May–Oct, Mon–Sat,
09.00–18.00; Sun, 11.00–19.00;
Oct–Apr, daily except Mon,
13.00–17.00
Admission charge

Derrynane Park
Open: all the time
Admission free

Cahergeal and Leacanabuaile
Open: all the time
Admission free

KILLARNEY
Tourist Information: Town Hall. Tel: (064) 31633

Killarney has a world-wide reputation for its stunning scenery. It is the one place in Ireland that most tourists want to see, yet the town itself is surprisingly small. Indeed, there seems to be little more than a main street, several side streets, a lot of shops selling souvenirs, and busy cafés and restaurants. The atmosphere, however, is one of excited expectation. There's hustle and bustle, noise and colour. Killarney, you see, is a base for tours around the wild and beautiful area which has become known as the Killarney Lake District. Drivers of jaunting-cars (horse and traps) offer tourists a trip with a difference. Visitors queue in the tourist information office eager to book their place on the many day and half-day excursions or to ask advice on planning their route.

One of the best ways to enjoy the splendour of the lakes is by an official organized day tour, bookable at the tourist information office. You travel by jaunting-car or coach to Kate Kearney's Cottage, an old coaching inn at the start of the breathtaking Gap of Dunloe with its panoramic views. The Gap is unsuitable for motorists so from here you either walk the seven scenic miles to the shore of the Upper Lake at Gearhameen or continue in a pony and trap. From the lake, boats take you through the narrow, winding stream known as the Long Range to the Meeting of the Waters where all three lakes meet. At the Old Weir Bridge you shoot the rapids at the approach to Muckross Lake (the Middle Lake), an exhilarating, if rather exhausting, experience. The boat trip ends by crossing Lough Leane (the Lower Lake), the largest of the three lakes, to the fourteenth-century Ross Castle. This lovely lake, shimmering in the sunlight, is dotted with small islets. The most beautiful is undoubtably Innisfallen with its lonely, ruined abbey founded in around 600 AD.

For motorists on a tight schedule, the route outlined below covers many of the main sights. Take the main Killarney to Kenmare road and then the first turn on the right to **Ross Castle**. Return to the main road and drive to the entrance of the recently renovated Muckross Abbey, noted as the burial place for four important Kerry families, namely the O'Donoghues, O'Sullivans, MacCarthys and also the MacGillicuddys (see page 84), after whom the high peaks beyond the

88

Purple Mountains are called. A mile away is **Muckross House**, a nineteenth-century manor house set in sheltered and sumptuous lakeside gardens. It is now a museum of Kerry folklife with many unusual items on show, together with displays on the geology and natural history of the area. In the basement there's a traditional craft centre where you can watch the craftspeople at work. You're now in the heart of the 25,000-acre **Killarney National Park** and Muckross House also serves as a visitor centre. To find out more about the park and the conservation work carried out, it's worth watching the audio-visual presentation.

The next stop before returning to Killarney is the **Torc Waterfall**, tucked away behind trees, a gushing, splashing, roaring marvel of nature that leaves you standing speechless in amazement. If you have time, do follow the footpath beside the fall – the views are spectacular. The main road leads onto another popular viewpoint, **Ladies View**, supposedly named after Queen Victoria's ladies-in-waiting who, on a State visit, were particularly pleased with the views over the Killarney Valley from this particular spot. Once back in Killarney, if you have time to spare, do drive up to Kate Kearney's Cottage at the start of the Gap of Dunloe (see above).

Ross Castle
Open: daily, dawn to dusk
(grounds only)
Admission free

Muckross Abbey
Open: daily, dawn to dusk
Admission free

Muckross House and Gardens
Tel: (064) 31440
Open: all year, mid-March to end June, daily, 10.00–19.00; July to end Aug, daily, 09.00–21.00; Sept to end Oct, daily, 10.00–19.00. Rest of year, daily, except Mon, 11.00–17.00
Admission charge

Killarney National Park
Tel: (064) 31947
Open: all year, daily, Easter–end May and Sept–Oct (inc), 09.00–19.00; June–Aug (inc) 09.00–21.00; Nov–Easter, 09.00–17.00
Admission free

Torc Waterfall
Open: daily, dawn to dusk
Admission free

Ladies View
Open: all the time
Admission free

A day spent exploring this rugged peninsula is an unforgettable experience. Memories linger long of the scarlet fuchsia hedges and wild orchids, the panoramic views, the changing light, varied mountain scenery, fascinating antiquities and rock formations dating back over 400 million years. It is predominantly an Irish-speaking area. The land in the far west is a 'Gaeltacht' known as Corca Dhuibhneknown. Here Irish Gaelic is spoken daily in the small villages and many of the old traditions, customs and crafts survive. At the small coastal village of Brandon you can still spot the skilled boatmen out in their curraghs, primitive boats made by stretching tarred canvas over a wooden frame.

It's best to leave a couple of days free to enjoy the peninsula, which stretches some 48 km westwards from Tralee, but at a push it can be covered in one long day. Try to choose a clear, bright day – or you will be among the many visitors who, thwarted by mist or continuous rain, see little further than their windscreen. There are many scenic routes for cyclists and horse-riders and for walkers, and there are footpaths and set walks, including the long-distance Dingle Way between Tralee and Dingle. There's so much of interest that it's a good idea to buy a guide from the tourist information office or bookshop to help you organize your route. A suggested tour for motorists is to take the road from Tralee to Dingle then on to the far west and back to Tralee via the Conor Pass. Towns and special features you will pass include Dingle (see below), Ventry Harbour (see p. 91), Fahan Monuments (see p. 91), Slea Head (see p. 92), Gallarus Oratory (see p. 92) and the Conor Pass (see p. 93).

DINGLE

This fishing centre where Irish Gaelic is spoken and, which claims the title of the most westerly town in Europe, is the principal place of the peninsula. It is a truly delightful spot with steep streets, shops and buildings full of character, colourful fishing boats coming in and out of the harbour, and an olde-worlde atmosphere that manages to be charming without being twee. It's an ideal place to stop for a picnic or possibly lunch in one of its good seafood restaurants. As you wander around look out for the house on the corner of John Street and Main Street. There's a story that it played a part in a plot to rescue Marie Antoinette after she had been captured during the French Revolution. Apparently the owner of the house, Count Rice, prepared all the rooms to receive her but his efforts were in vain. Marie Antoinette refused to travel so far.

Dingle is set amidst fine scenery and is bounded on three sides by hills. To the north towers Mount Brandon, the second highest mountain in Ireland at 953 m. To the east runs the Slieve Mish range of mountains. And to the west is a coastal plain, dotted with hamlets where the Gaelic culture still thrives.

VENTRY HARBOUR
Nr Ventry

Around 5 km west of Dingle is Ventry. As you leave this small village, take time to enjoy the fine views of Ventry Harbour, scene of an ancient romantic tale, 'Cath Fionntra' (The Battle of Ventry Strand). This romantic tale, found in a fifteenth-century manuscript, tells of how the King of the World, Daire Donn, and his followers tried to invade Ireland but after a year and a day were defeated on the sands by the brave standing army of Fionn Mac Cumhaill, the legendary third-century hero.

FAHAN MONUMENTS
Ventry to Slea Head Road

The peninsula is particularly rich in archaeological remains. Indeed, excavations have identified over 2,000 monuments, mainly prehistoric and early Christian. The Fahan group of monuments, situated on the Ventry to Slea Head road, are probably the greatest collection of antiquities in all Ireland. Your first sight of them will be signs pointing you to the Beehive Huts. There are over 400 'clochans', drystone beehive-shaped cells or huts, and it's well worth walking up the grassy slopes to take a look at these remarkable early dwelling places. But don't be surprised if the door of one of the nearby whitewashed cottages opens and a local resident asks for an entrance fee, you are on their land, after all. Other monuments in this group include Dunbeg Fort, an Iron Age promontory fort, cave dwellings, standing and inscribed stones, earthern ring forts and two sculptured crosses.

Open: all the time
Admission free

SLEA HEAD

You may well have already admired the wild and beautiful scenery around Slea Head without knowing its location. This is the setting for the film *Ryan's Daughter* and you can still see the remains of the schoolhouse used during the filming, standing on a cliff looking out to sea. Slea Head, the most westerly headland in Ireland, is also noted for its splendid views. Look out to the Blaskets, a mass of red limestone islands 2 km from the western tip of peninsula. The largest of the islands, the Great Blasket, was occupied until the 1950s and has been home for many famous Irish writers who gained inspiration from the remote setting. Many of the islands have been occupied since far back in time; proof lies in the excavated remains of hermitages and early fortresses. Nearer to the Head, the sea is scattered with rocks. You can't miss the Tearaght. The largest and most impressive, it stands 183 m high and covers 47 acres.

GALLARUS ORATORY
Nr Dingle

This early Christian church represents a quite remarkable feat of construction, an almost perfect piece of dry stone work. Probably dating back to the eighth century, it is still completely watertight. Visitors are welcome to explore inside. It is built in the shape of an upturned boat and has walls over 1 m thick at their base. A short drive away a later style of ecclesiastical architecture is found at the twelfth-century Hiberno-Romanesque Kilmalkedar Church. Among its treasures are a crudely carved alphabet stone, an early seventh-century cross and an ogham stone. Nearby is a track known as the Saint's Road, supposedly laid by St Brendan, patron saint of Kerry. The road leads to his sixth-century oratory (remains of which can still be seen, together with a number of stone huts) on the summit of the Brandon Mountain and has been traced in many great pilgrimages. Mount Brandon, scene of four air crashes in the Second World War, is named after St Brendan. The mountainous range can be explored by visitors but do take sensible precautions. The best place to start your climb is at Cloghane, a village set on an inlet of Brandon Bay.

Open: all the time
Admission free

CONOR PASS

Cloghane can be reached by crossing the highest mountain pass in Ireland, the Conor Pass, which runs over the Brandon range from Dingle towards Castlegregory. The road climbs to an exhilarating height of 457 m and then winds around the base of the cliffs and drops into a mass of boulder-strewn nothingness. Stop at the top to admire the views: to the north are the fishing bays of Brandon and Tralee and beyond is the mouth of the Shannon. The bays, separated by the sandy Rough Point peninsula with its fine beaches, are famed for their fishing; catches from tropical and sub-tropical Arctic seas have been recorded. To the south is Dingle Bay and the outskirts of Dingle town and, in a deep valley below the road (if you dare to look), are a number of lakes that shine like jewels amid the cliffs.

BLENNERVILLE WINDMILL
Blennerville, Tralee

The small town of Blennerville, just south of Tralee, was a meeting place for emigrants during the Great Famine. They gathered there to wait for a place on one of the crowded emigrant ships that sailed from the pier. Today, it is best known for its windmill. Built in around 1780, it stands 21 m high and is one of Europe's largest traditional windmills. Now restored and in full working order, it houses many fascinating exhibits on the history of both the windmill and the area as a whole. At the time of writing, the surrounding buildings were being converted to provide a craft centre and visitor facilities. Eventually it is planned that Blennerville will be linked to the nearby seaside town of Fenit by a steamboat service.

Open: Mar–Oct, Mon–Sat,
10.00–18.00; Sun, 14.00–18.00
Admission charge

TRALEE
Tourist Information: 32 The Mall. Tel: (066) 21288

This market town is probably best known for the annual international festival, the highlight of which is the 'Rose of Tralee' beauty contest. Girls of Irish origin come from all over the world to compete for the much-coveted title. Held in late August/early September, the whole week is a traditional farewell to summer with music, song and festivities. Tralee, the county town of Kerry, is situated 3 km above the point where the River Lee flows into Tralee Bay, hence its name Traigh Li, 'Beach of the River Lee'. Tralee has a long and varied history but sadly two fires in 1643 and 1691 destroyed its older buildings so the visitor has to rely on local guidebooks to fill in the details. One of the points of interest in the town is Denny Street with its fine Georgian buildings; however, its main attraction is its beautiful setting and good position as a touring base for both the Dingle Peninsula (see p. 90) and the Ring of Kerry (see p. 84).

SIAMSA, THE NATIONAL FOLK
THEATRE OF IRELAND
Siamsa Tire Theatre, Godfrey Place, Tralee. Tel: (066) 23055

For lovers of folk theatre, Siamsa is undoubtedly one of the most inspirational performances of its kind. Founded in 1968 by a Catholic priest, Pat Ahern, who grew up on a farm in North Kerry, the theatre is his way of preserving the traditional country customs and music of his youth. The idea behind Siamsa is to recapture the spirit of a past way of life by recreating on stage some of the everyday activities of a typical rural family years ago in Gaelic-speaking Ireland. Although folk theatre is not to everyone's taste, Siamsa has proved so successful that it is in constant demand in overseas countries and regularly tours abroad after the popular summer season at Tralee.

Dressed in colourful native costume, the cast of about twenty-seven players, aged from eleven to seventy, exude endless amounts of energy and enthusiasm for their work. They perform a series of intricate mime dances, centred around different farmyard activities, to the music of pipes, flute and fiddle. Each job on the farm has its own song and dance, there's a feeding song for the chickens, a milking song for the cows and a sharpening song for the scythe. And country customs such as the fire ceremonies on the eve of May Day and superstitions such as the blessing of the butter churn, when everyone in the house took a turn, are brought to life through music, dance and song.

Open: June–Sept. For performance
dates and times contact the theatre
Admission charge

ARDFERT CATHEDRAL, CHURCHES
AND FRIARY
Ardfert

Eight kilometres northwest of Tralee is the small town of Ardfert, properly known as Ardfert-Brendan after St Brendan, who founded a monastery here in the sixth century. Like so many Irish saints, tales and legends abound around Brendan the navigator (483–578) who is reputed to have reached America. He was born in the neighbourhood but the exact whereabouts depends on who you talk to; the most probable place, however, is the small port of Fenit, across Tralee Bay.

There are extensive medieval remains. The present cathedral stands on the site of an earlier stone church which was struck by lightning in 1046. The cathedral, which dates back to the twelfth century, has an impressive and much-photographed Romanesque doorway and inside there are effigies of two thirteenth-century bishops. Nearby are the remains of the Romanesque Temple-na-Hoe (of the Virgin) and the small fifteenth-century Temple-na-Griffin. Look out for the two wyverns (winged dragons with eagle's feet) sculpted in a window jamb inside the north wall. The figures, often mistaken for griffins, represent evil devouring itself. There's no trace of the round tower that once stood on the monastic site.

A few hundred yards away are the ruins of Ardfert Friary, believed to have been founded in around 1253. Although the building has been much altered over the years, you can still see the Gothic chancel. Among its other features are the fine south window and beautiful cloister.

Open: all the time
Admission free

LISTOWEL RACES

For regulars at Listowel race week the sight of local children standing ankle deep in water beneath the bridge is a familiar one. However, newcomers look on in surprise as the children shout up to passers-by 'throw me down something' and hold out cardboard boxes to catch the falling coins. It's a tradition, like so much at the famous five-day September Listowel race meeting, that goes back years. The races are part of the Harvest Festival of Ireland week and a carnival atmosphere fills the town as locals and holidaymakers come from miles around to place a few bob on the horses and join in what has become a major social event. Betting is hard and furious both on-course and off with banknotes changing hands at an alarming pace, but despite the hard gambling there's a friendly ambience. Everyone is most definitely determined to have a good time, winners or losers. The drink flows freely and laughter rises from all quarters.

Listowel is famed for its literary associations both past and present and each week in June there's a Writers' Week with workshops, lectures and short courses. Listowel is also a popular venue for the Fleadh Cheoil Na hEireann, the National Festival of Irish music. Among the town's other attractions are the two Gothic-style churches facing each other over the central square, the ruined fifteenth-century castle, the Listowel Arms Hotel where James Stewart Parnell made one of his last public appearances in 1891, the fine shop-fronts, and the ornamental plasterwork.

For exact dates of the races and Writers' Week contact: Cork/Kerry Tourism, Tourist House, Grand Parade, Cork. Tel: (021) 273251.

BALLYBUNION

This lively little seaside resort with its amusing-sounding name acts like a magnet for golfers who come in their coachloads to test their skills on the town's two demanding 18-hole courses. Set high on a spectacular range of sandhills, both courses offer not only excellent golf but also splendid views over the sandy strand lapped by the Atlantic Ocean, a whitewash of breaking waves on a windy day.

However, for non-golfers there are other attractions. Energetic visitors will enjoy the invigorating cliff walk, which takes you over Ballybunion's caves (at low tide some can be entered on foot) and at sunset provides a quite dramatic viewpoint for the ruin of Ballybunion Castle. On a summer's day sun-seekers may prefer to find a space among the parasols and spread their towels on the popular sands or take a picnic to a quieter spot beside the Cashen River. For the more adventurous, Ballybunion boasts the only seaweed baths in Ireland. There are two sets of baths on Ladies' Strand where you can immerse yourself in the steaming seaweed known as bladder wrack, freshly picked from the rocks, which gives out a thick, oily, slippery substance once in water. These baths, long reputed to have medicinal, beautifying and relaxing powers, are a marvellous cure for a hangover!

Seaweed Baths
Open: June–Sept daily. Times vary
Admission charge

Castle and Cave
Open: all the time
Admission free

COUNTY LIMERICK

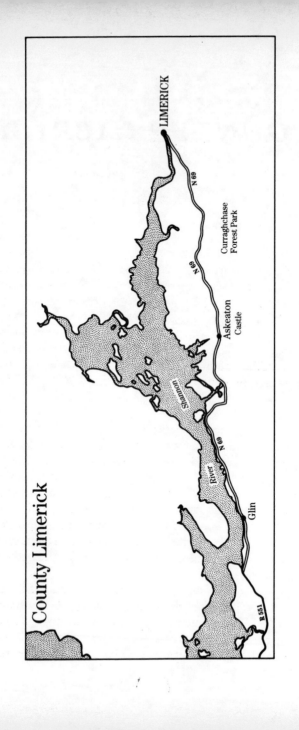

COUNTY LIMERICK

County Limerick is roughly rectangular in shape and most of it is inland. However, the relatively small section which is fringed by the sea spreads prettily along the south side of the Shannon estuary. The estuary is popular with sailors as it offers reasonably sheltered conditions, and as it has been fiercely defended over the centuries there are numerous ruined castles to explore. There are also many remains from more ancient times, most notably inland at Lough Gur. This is reputed to be one of the most important archaeological sites in Ireland with evidence of hunter-fisher folk dating back 3,000 years. In addition, on the lough's shores once stood the old Viking city of Limerick.

Geologically, County Limerick is very varied. The oldest rocks in the region are Silurian, they were formed some 400 million years ago. They form the core of the Galty, Ballyhoura and Slievefelim mountains, which are topped by large deposits of old red sandstone. Volcanic rock can also be found in the area. The soil of the region, formed from such a wide range of rocks, together with substantial glacial deposits, is very fertile. It supports verdant pasturage, in particular the rich plain of the Golden Vale, which runs northwest of the Galty mountains. Not surprisingly, Limerick is Ireland's premier dairying county.

At the point where the River Shannon becomes tidal stands the historic city of Limerick, the region's county town. Attempts are being made at urban regeneration, though economic problems remain. Much is being done to revitalize the region by the Shannon Free Airport Development Company, who co-ordinate and promote the notion of tourism in the area; it is under their auspices that such entertainments as medieval banquets are flourishing.

Today the county of Limerick offers visitors glimpses of the distant past, the more recent past and even a few indications of how things might progress. And much of this variety may be found along its coast – from long-established settlements to unspoiled forest walks which reach right down to the water's edge.

GLIN CASTLE
Glin. Tel: (068) 34173

The exterior of this eighteenth-century castle overlooking the Shannon is fairly plain, although battlements, Gothic details and a surprisingly large number of windows do give it a certain character. It's the interior that people come to see. Indeed, as soon as you set foot inside it's like walking into a different world. Glin Castle is the residence of the twenty-ninth Knight of Glin, an Irish art-historian, writer on architecture and also a man of impeccable taste who has obviously taken great pride in the restoration of his mansion. The rooms are exquisitely furnished and decorated and among the most notable features are the stucco ceilings, an extraordinary double 'flying' staircase and a fine collection of eighteenth-century Irish furniture, paintings and family portraits.

The present owner's family have held land in the area for around 700 years. The original medieval castle was largely destroyed in 1600 after what records show to be a valiant effort to resist an attack. The unexciting ruins of the tower house just outside the village are all that remain of this once-great castle. The new castle was built in 1789 by the twenty-fourth knight immediately after his marriage. His son, strongly influenced by the Gothic style, added the battlements and west wing in 1815. It was also his idea to build the pepperpot gate-lodges. One of the charming lodges, on the main Tarbert road, is now a restaurant and shop selling crafts and curios.

Castle
Open: mid-May to mid-June, 10.00–12.00, 14.00–16.00 or by arrangement
Admission charge

Glin Castle Shop
Tel: (068) 34188
Open: Apr–Oct (inc)

ASKEATON CASTLE AND FRIARY
Askeaton

The small town of Askeaton on the River Deel is dominated by the haunting ruins of the fifteenth-century tower of Desmond Castle. Standing on a rocky inlet in the river, the imposing tower is on the site of a previous castle built around 1199. Although it is far from complete, lovers of old buildings will find much of interest here. Features to note in the tower include the fireplace on the third floor and many of the windows. To the west is a splendid medieval banqueting hall measuring 9 m by 27 m with beautifully carved windows and blind arcading.

The remains of the Franciscan friary stand on the east side of the river. The old friary church, with its fine windows, was built at the time of the friary's foundation in the late fourteenth century. Most of the other buildings date back to 1420–40. The cloister is particularly well preserved; note the marble arches and figure of St Francis in the northeast corner. Above the cloister is the dormitory and, to the south, the refectory where you can still see the niche for the reader to stand in during mealtimes. The friary was used until the beginning of the eighteenth century, although it was plundered in 1579 and some of the friars massacred.

If you have time, it's worth exploring the village itself. Look out for the thirteenth-century St Mary's Church and the grave of the Irish poet and author Aubrey Thomas de Vere, who was buried there in 1902.

Open: at any reasonable hour (castle key from house beside the gate)   **Admission free**

CURRAGHCHASE FOREST PARK
Off N69

If you find yourself inspired by the tranquil beauty as you wander through this 600-acre park, then you're not alone. These woods were a favourite stamping ground of Aubrey Thomas de Vere, well-respected Irish poet and author, who was born at Curraghchase in

1814. The de Vere family have been associated with the area for over 300 years. The mansion they built as their residence in the mid-seventeenth century was destroyed by fire in 1941 and only the outer shell now remains. However, the grounds they landscaped with lake and woodlands can still be enjoyed today. Set aside a good few hours as it's not a place to be rushed, you need time to appreciate your surroundings.

The extensive park with so much space to run around in and interesting pockets to explore has become a popular venue for family picnics and Sunday walks in the countryside. It's also the perfect setting to test your knowledge of nature so take binoculars and camera and try identifying the different trees and shrubs, spotting the birds and following the tracks of wild animals. To help there's a useful guidebook on sale giving detailed notes of what to look for on your rambles. There are also signposted walks of varying lengths and a trail through the arboretum with its many exotic trees.

Open: all the time
Admission free

LIMERICK
Tourist Information: The Granary, St Michael Street.
(061) 317522

Now the fourth largest city in Ireland, Limerick dates back to the fourth century when it was a Norse settlement. However, Brian Boru invaded it in 964 AD and made it his capital. Limerick's history continued to be turbulent – it was captured by the Anglo Normans in the twelfth century, retaken by Donal O'Brien, and fell once more to the Anglo Normans. It became a prosperous and important English trading centre which was taken by the Scots, then sacked by the O'Briens. In 1651, during Cromwellian times, Limerick was taken after being under siege for six months. In 1690 it was once again under siege, this time from William of Orange.

Present-day Limerick has three main sections: Irish Town, English Town and Newtown Perry. At its centre is a marketplace void of tourists but full of life. However, as you start to wander through the streets and alleyways it becomes all too clearly a run-down city with all the usual problems of urban decay. Nevertheless, Limerick is worth visiting for the wealth of history which is locked in its buildings, streets and bridges.

King John's Castle, Nicholas Street. A short walk from St Mary's are the remains of King John's Castle. Built around 1200, its gatehouse, towers and curtain walls survive. Dark, murky and uninviting, the castle is worth braving if only for the magnificent view from the roof of its highest tower. The city of Limerick is spread out around it and the wide waters of the Shannon wash its walls far below.

Open: mid-June to mid-Sept daily,   **Admission charge**
10.00–18.00 (at other times key is
with caretaker)

Limerick Museum, St John's Square. Limerick Museum is an excellent place to find out more about the city and a good starting place for a visitor. This neat, informative collection covers all periods of history from the Stone Age onwards, including local aspects of national independence. On display are all sorts of items, such as Limerick silver and lace, along with some atmospheric old photographs.

Open: Tues–Sat, 10.00–13.00;
14.15–17.00
Admission free

St John's Cathedral, Cathedral Place. Across the square from Limerick Museum is St John's Cathedral. Built in the mid-nineteenth century it is Gothic revival in style with a painted ceiling and colourful stained glass. At 85 m, St John's also boasts the highest spire in Ireland.

Open: daily
Admission free

St Mary's Cathedral, Patrick Street. When compared with St John's, St Mary's Cathedral seems somewhat drab. However, history is on St Mary's side because it dates back to the twelfth century. Look out for the carved misericords, which are said to be unique in Ireland. Of interest too is the leper's squint – a hole through which the lepers of Limerick once received Holy Communion.

Open: daily
Admission free

Son et lumière show, nightly, June–Sept, admission charge

COUNTY CLARE

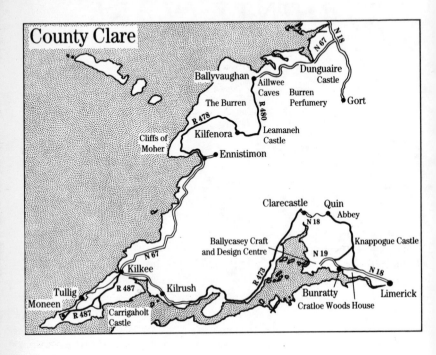

COUNTY CLARE

County Clare takes its name from the Irish An Clar, which means a level surface or plain. There is a great stretch of flat land through the centre of Clare, but its coastline boasts many high rugged crags, including the dramatic Cliffs of Moher. However, for the visitor leaving Limerick and entering Clare, the land is initially flat and barren. The route up to remote Loop Head – the most westerly point on the peninsula – is frequently made impassable by the washing of the sea. The feeling here is one of desolation; few tourists follow the narrow, pot-hole pocked lanes of this region. Further north Clare becomes more obviously picturesque and consequently tour buses are not uncommon. A major tourist attraction is the Burren, a vast limestone phenomenon which is unique in Europe.

Clare has a reputation for good music. The music-making centres around impromptu gatherings in small pubs where anyone who can play a tune or sing a ballad does a turn. Such gatherings vary from pub to pub and from night to night, but you're sure to stumble upon this popular entertainment quickly enough. Although a great deal of this still-living traditional music has been noted down, much of it has never been recorded anywhere – Ireland simply has a plethora of good music. In May Clare hosts the Fleadh Nue, an annual music and song festival which evolved from the All-Ireland event. Although more formal than most gatherings, it is an enjoyable showcase for traditional Irish music, dancing and singing.

CRATLOE WOODS HOUSE
Cratloe. Tel: (061) 87306

A short driveway off the busy Limerick–Shannon dual carriageway leads to Cratloe Woods House, easily recognized by its stunning crushed strawberry colour. You gain entry by ringing a bell and waiting. Eventually footsteps are heard a long way away, gradually they come nearer and the vibrant blue door is opened. Once welcomed indoors, you're in a different world. One of the few roofed examples of a traditional Irish longhouse to survive, Cratloe is full of atmosphere. It was built in the seventeenth century by the O'Briens – historically the leading family of the region – and is still lived in by members of the same family. They use lions, the symbol of power and royalty, in their Stafford-O'Brien coat of arms. Visits to the house take the form of a guided tour, which more often than not starts with an invitation to take some tea and sample home-baked scones (charge). Although organized primarily for security reasons, the guided tour has a personal quality; just for a while you can imagine that you are a guest at Cratloe being shown around by a genial host. Most of the furniture, paintings and mementos are of a domestic nature rather than of great historical importance, but this in no way detracts from their appeal. There are family oil paintings, 2,000-year-old Egyptian beads (left over from the days when the O'Briens traded in distant lands), and even a Victorian vacuum cleaner. Outside, the River Shannon rushes by at the end of the gardens, which are gradually being restored, and there's a small cobbled farmyard with horse-drawn farm machinery on display.

Open: June to mid-Sept, Mon–Sat,
14.00–18.00
Admission charge

BUNRATTY CASTLE AND FOLK PARK
Off N18. Tel: (061) 361511

Bunratty Castle was built by Sioda MacNamara around 1450. During the fifteenth and sixteenth centuries it was an important stronghold of the O'Briens. Its rectangular keep is said to be the finest of its kind in Ireland. High, imposing and protected by a drawbridge, the keep contains a number of interesting rooms. Most spectacular of all is undoubtedly the splendid Great Hall. This was originally the banquet hall and audience chamber of the Earls of Thomond. Its floor is paved with marble squares and its furnishings date back mainly to the fifteenth and sixteenth centuries. There is a particularly fine oak chest which is early Gothic and a ceremonial drinking horn of the same period. Other rooms to explore inside the keep include the kitchen, guard room, chapel, solar, bedroom and robing room.

Once you've seen the castle, there's a large folk park to explore. The park offers the opportunity to look inside some of the different sorts of cottages which dot the Irish landscape. A few of the buildings are real cottages which have been carefully dismantled and then rebuilt in the grounds of the castle; others are merely reconstructions. Parts of the park lack atmosphere and authenticity – it is, for example, hard to imagine that the village street ever looked so picture-postcard quaint, or that the whitewashed cottage ever had so many perfect roses twining around its doorway. Nevertheless, there's plenty to see and to learn. There's a byre dwelling from County Mayo which gives an insight into the cramped conditions from a time when humans and animals shared the same building; a blacksmith's forge from County Limerick, typical of a rural forge; and a flour mill reconstructed on the basis of excavations in County Cork (do ask to see it in operation). In contrast to the poorer dwellings, Georgian Bunratty House, on a small hill above the park, seems spacious and comfortable – it is of the type once occupied by minor gentry.

Open: daily, 09.30–17.00 (last admission 16.15); May–Aug, park open until 19.00 (last admission 18.15)

Admission charge
Medieval Banquets: bookings.
Tel: (061) 61788

BALLYCASEY CRAFT AND DESIGN CENTRE
Ballycasey, Shannon, Off N18. Tel: (061) 62105

The one-time courtyard of eighteenth-century Ballycaseymore House has been clinically converted into a craft and design centre and is used by a wide range of skilled workers. This is a workplace, and all the items you can see being made are for sale. However there is no pressure to buy, you are very welcome to browse and if you have a question don't be afraid to voice it. The craftspeople who work here do change from time to time but you can usually count on seeing a dozen or so on any visit, including a potter, a weaver, a jewellery-maker and a fashion designer.

Open: all year, Mon–Sat,
10.00–17.00
Admission free

MEDIEVAL BANQUET
Knappogue Castle, Nr Sixmilebridge. Tel: (061) 61788

The cover of darkness must be the best time to experience the atmosphere of any castle, and Knappogue is no exception. Burning torches light its entrance and maidens with mead-filled goblets welcome visitors. The banquet may not be authentic, but it is entertaining. Around 150 guests dine at each sitting (there are two most nights each lasting two hours exactly). The set menu is neither typically medieval nor particularly Irish: soup, smoked salmon, chicken and plenty of cheap wine. Still, the service is friendly and the pageant which is offered as the evening's entertainment is surprisingly good. The lads and lasses who have been diligently presenting plates of food and topping up goblets are a talented crew. Donning shawls and hats they take to the stage and with wit, song and dance present a much-abridged version of Irish history. The pageant over, it's time to leave – though not through the imposing main entrance; this time it's out into a back courtyard and into the car park via the gift shop, which

Right: Achill Head,
County Mayo
(The Slide File)

Below: Westport House,
County Mayo
(Bord Fáilte)

'The Cascade' formation at Aillwee Caves, County Clare *(Courtesy of The Aillwee Cave Co. Ltd)*

The Burren, County Clare *(Bord Fáilte)*

Above: Siamsa Tíre, The National Folk Theatre of Ireland, Tralee, County Kerry
(Frank Lewis, Killarney)

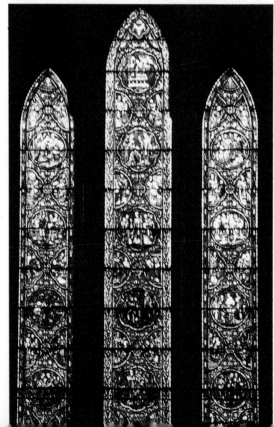

Right: The window in the South Transept, St Patrick's Cathedral, Dublin *(Courtesy of St Patrick's Cathedral)*

Left: High Cross, Monasterboice, County Louth
(The Slide File)

Below: Mizen Head, County
Cork *(The Slide File)*

Right: Avoca River, County Wicklow *(The Slide File)*

Below: Round Tower, Ardmore Monastic Ruins, County Waterford
(Bord Fáilte)

Opposite: St Kevin's Kitchen and Church, Glendalough, County Wicklow
(The Slide File)

Right: St Gobban's Church, Port Bradden, County Antrim
(Northern Ireland Tourist Board)

Below: Hezlett House, County Londonderry
(NITB)

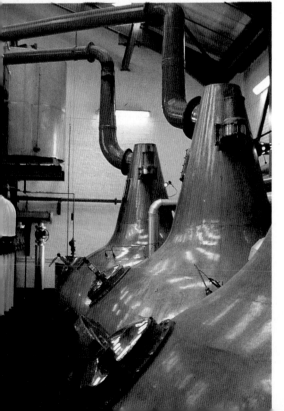

Above: The Silent Valley Reservoir and Mourne Mountains, County Down *(NITB)*

Left: The 'Pot Stills' in the Old Bushmills Distillery, County Antrim *(Courtesy of the 'Old Bushmills' Distillery Co. Ltd)*

obligingly stays open until the very last paying guest leaves the premises.

During the daytime, Knappogue has a totally different ambience. Its recently restored rooms include the great hall, a chamber used by the Princes of Thomond and the Lords of Clancullen. Knappogue was one of the forty-two castles built by the once-powerful MacNamara clan who for more than a thousand years ruled the territory of Clancullen in Clare.

Open: daily, Easter to end Sept,
09.30–17.30. Banquets May–Sept
Admission charge

QUIN ABBEY
Quin

Though ruined, Quin Abbey is reputed to be one of the best-preserved abbeys in Ireland. Situated on a pretty river bank in the small, quiet village of Quin, the abbey is a tranquil place in which to linger. However, this was not always a peaceful spot. The abbey is built within the ruins of a Norman castle, which was destroyed in 1286. Small fragments of the castle can still be seen in and around the ruins of the abbey, which include a well-preserved, elegantly buttressed cloister as well as the nave, chancel and tower. A Franciscan order was founded here in 1402 by Sioda MacNamara, but was suppressed in 1541. The Franciscan community was officially disbanded in 1651; however, the last monk died in 1820 and is buried within the abbey walls.

Wandering through the abbey ruins today you are likely to see fresh graves with colourful floral tributes as it is still used as a burial ground.

Open: daily (or key with caretaker)
Admission free

CARRIGAHOLT CASTLE
Carrigaholt

Carrigaholt Castle is in a tiny fishing village on the north bank of the Shannon estuary. All that remains is an astonishingly narrow keep whose interior is around 3 m wide. Nevertheless, this slim five-storey tower does command a good vantage point once prized by the MacMahons who built it in the fifteenth century. Today it's a haven for grazing cows and offers a good view over the small pier.

Open: all the time
Admission free

THE LITTLE ARK
Our Lady Star Of The Sea Church, Moneen

The modern church in Moneen seems uninviting to a visitor in search of the old and the picturesque. Yet it contains a truly thought-provoking relic – The Little Ark. This small weather-beaten wooden construction, which looks something like a cross between a garden shed and a bathing box, was used last century by the parish priest, Father Meehan, to celebrate Mass. From 1852–7 it was forbidden to practise the Catholic faith anywhere other than the no-man's-land of the sea-shore, and Father Meehan used this Little Ark for Sunday services. Whatever the weather, poor, often starving, families gathered on the shore around the ark to hear Mass, to be married and to be baptized.

Open: daily
Admission free

BRIDGES OF ROSS
Nr Tullig

As spectacular in their own way as the Cliffs of Moher (see page 116) yet relatively undiscovered, the Bridges of Ross are remarkable natural rock formations. Two large bridges (one partially worn away) have been formed by the incessant washing of the powerful Atlantic Ocean. The tides have shaped the rock strata so perfectly that the bridges look deceptively man-made. You can walk over their dramatic arches and peer into the green-black water far below. Beyond the bridges great slabs of grey stone, which slide down into the foaming sea, provide good vantage points for fishermen as well as a multitude of crevices for small plants.

Open: all the time
Admission free

ENNISTYMON

If you need to stock up on provisions, the small market town of Ennistymon is the place to make for. The town's colourful shop-fronts are quite famous (they sometimes feature on posters of Ireland). These, along with their often traditional interiors, make shopping a pleasure. Less pretty than most, but definitely not to be missed, is Unglert's Bakery (on the main street). Unglert's home-baked breads – soda, wholemeal, soya and rye – are a real treat.

Ennistymon grew up around an O'Brien castle which was built here in 1588, but it is now dominated by a twentieth-century church. This new church is sited near the ruins of a church which date from 1778. However, a much, much earlier church, St Mainchin's, is known to have stood here in 580 AD.

Today most visitors enjoy a walk beside the River Cullenagh, which forms a fast-flowing cascade in the heart of the town.

CLIFFS OF MOHER
Nr R478

Choose a clear day to visit the Cliffs of Moher and you will be rewarded with a spectacular cliff-face panorama; choose a cloudy day and you'll be disappointed as thick sea mists drop down low over the cliffs and obscure them from view. The 204 m high precipice has been developed to attract large numbers of tourists (there's a visitor centre, information desk, shop, café and large car park) and it's easy to see its appeal. The cliffs extend some 10 km, but most visitors just make the short climb up to O'Brien's Tower. The tower was built in 1835, on the highest section of the cliffs, by Sir Cornelius O'Brien, MP, as an observation point for 'strangers visiting the magnificent scenery of this neighbourhood'. On a clear day, and perhaps with the aid of the telescope on the roof of the tower, you can see as far as Loop Head, the Kerry Mountains, the Aran Islands and the Twelve Bens of Connemara.

If you're a keen birdwatcher, bring your binoculars – guillemots, razorbills, shags, kittiwakes and puffins can all be spotted here during the nesting season.

Cliffs
Open: all the time; Visitor Centre, daily, Mar to end Oct, 10.00–18.00
Admission free

O'Brien's Tower
Open: daily 1 May to early Sept, 10.00–18.00
Admission charge

THE BURREN DISPLAY CENTRE
Kilfenora. Tel: (065) 88030

Unless you're a geologist, you may do well to visit the Burren Display Centre before you venture into the outstanding geographical feature of the Clare landscape. The beauty of the Burren (see below) can of course by enjoyed by anyone, but it does seem to add an extra dimension if you understand what you are seeing.

The centre is run as a co-operative by the town of Kilfenora – some 400 local people are shareholders. It is a valiant effort to create both a resource for visitors and employment for locals. Apart from its shop, the centre offers two main attractions. There is an audio-visual presentation which provides a basic introduction to the Burren. However, its ten-minute duration is something of a trial as the transmission quality (at the time of writing) is poor. There follows an excellent short lecture during which even the most well-informed visitor is likely to learn a thing or two.

Adjacent to the centre is Kilfenora Cathedral. A monastery was built on this site during the sixth century and the present ruined building dates back to 1190. In the graveyard and nearby field there are four twelfth-century High Crosses. Look out for the one known as the Doorty Cross – it is thought to symbolize friendship between two tribes.

Centre
Open: daily, mid-Mar to end Oct, 10.00–17.00; July to Aug 10.00–19.00
Admission charge

Kilfenora Cathedral
Open: daily
Admission free

THE BURREN

The 500 square kilometres of the Burren leave most visitors gasping. It has been described as a lunar landscape because the first impression given is one of barrenness. For as far as the eye can see there are grey, seemingly lifeless limestone formations. Indeed, the name Burren comes from Boireann, which means a rocky place. Of this unique place Sir John Betjeman wrote, 'Stony seaboard fair and foreign/Stony hills poured over space/Stony outcrop of the Burren/ Stones in every fertile place.' However, in amongst the stones there is a wealth of plant life. Sharp-eyed visitors may spot a rare orchid along with maidenhair fern, rock rose, red helleborine and mountain avens. Multicoloured lichens thrive (an indication of the pollution-free atmosphere), along with hosts of butterflies, moths and birds. Animals such as foxes, stoats, squirrels and badgers abound but are less easy to spot than the sure-footed wild goats which have made the Burren their kingdom. They graze on the thick areas of low hazel – the only tree to grow in the area.

The Burren may seem a daunting place for humans to live, but axe heads dating back 7,000 years have been found here. Stone Age settlers lived in this region between 2,000 and 3,000 years ago – their wedge-shaped tombs, cairns and dolmens can still be seen. Best known is the Gleninsheen wedge-tomb near Aillwee Cave. A beautiful gold collar, said to be one of the finest discovered from the Bronze Age, was found here in 1930. Ring forts from the Bronze Age have also survived, take a look at Cahercommaun, Ballykinvarga and Cahermacnaghten.

Open: all the time
Admission free

LEAMANEH CASTLE
Nr Kilfenora

Situated on the edge of the Burren and built of local stone, the ruins of Leamaneh Castle are very much part of the rock-strewn landscape. The majestic facade is a strange juxtaposition of two different building styles. Part is a grand but nevertheless domestic building, and part is a tall square tower of the type common in Ireland. It is said that Maire Rua O'Brien got rid of her husband over its battlements! Today only the shell survives and a spiral of five flights of stairs which lead up to a small roof area. The view in every direction is worth the climb though it's definitely not for anyone who suffers from vertigo.

The land around the castle is still farmed to a large extent as it was hundreds of years ago. The farmers practise transhumance, moving their cattle from summer meadows to hilltop 'winterages' to take advantage of the winter Burren grass.

Open: all the time
Admission free

AILLWEE CAVES
Ballyvaughan. Tel: (065) 77036/77067

There are no rivers or streams running through the Burren, yet the area receives plenty of rain. So where does the water go? The answer is, it disappears through fissures in the rocks and reappears miles away outside the Burren area. The underground waterways, which range in size from merest trickles to fast-flowing subterranean rivers, have carved out numerous caves including the spectacular ones at Aillwee.

Aillwee caves were discovered earlier this century by a local herds-man searching for his dog. A brave man he must have been indeed, as he explored the cave for about a quarter of a mile by candlelight. The underground route extended some 1,036 m into the mountain and has now been fully developed for visits by the public.

All visits are by guided tour. They last about 30 minutes and it can get cold deep underground even during the summer. The guides are very knowledgeable and able to answer most questions about the geology of the caves and the surrounding area. They point out the different types of stalactites and stalagmites and explain how they were formed. The most spectacular part of the caves is perhaps the Cascade Chamber. Here a seemingly frozen waterfall shimmers in the cave's dramatic lighting. The cascade is a large deposit of crystalline calcite which has coated the rock. It was formed by a trickle of water constantly running down the wall of the cave slowly making a sheet of calcite. Pure calcite is white, but in the Aillwee caves it is stained yellowy-orange by iron compounds.

The caves at Aillwee once provided refuge for animals, most notably bears. The bones of a brown bear together with bear pits and claw marks have all been discovered. As bears have been extinct in Ireland for over 1,000 years, the findings are thought to be very old. Life in the caves today is restricted to visitors and hibernating animals such as foxes, badgers and bats.

Open: daily, summer, 10.00–19.00; mid-July to mid-Aug, 10.00–20.00; winter, 10.00–17.00. Tours every 15 mins, duration 30 mins

Admission charge

BALLYVAUGHAN

Sandwiched between the edge of the Burren and the sea, Bally-vaughan is an attractive fishing village which has expanded just a little to meet the demands of tourism. Beside the small harbour a cluster of whitewashed cottages are holiday homes, the main street boasts a good restaurant, a workshop development thrives. Yet none of this seems to have spoilt the tranquillity here; visitors simply blend into the way of life.

Burren Pottery. Tel: (065) 77072. Adjoining Original Textiles (see below) is Burren Pottery. Here potter Andrew Russell can be seen throughout the summer making a range of pots and dishes which have proved popular with tourists. However, visit outside the main tourist season and you may catch sight of him producing one-off pieces of Raku. Raku is an ancient Japanese technique used originally for making tea ceremony bowls; Andrew uses it to form unique sculptural pieces.

Open: Easter to end Sept,
Mon–Sat, 09.30–18.00
Admission free

Manus Enamels. Tel: (065) 77029. Situated in the centre of Bally-vaughan above Claire's restaurant (which specializes in such delights as crab claws cooked in garlic butter, followed perhaps by salmon steaks, all served at intimate candle-lit tables) is a tiny gallery and workshop known as Manus Enamels. Here Dubliner Manus Walsh creates beautiful enamel works featuring Celtic motifs such as the Burren dolmens.

Open: daily, Easter–Oct,
10.00–19.00
Admission free

Original Textiles. Tel: (065) 77061. In a workshop near to Manus Enamels, Kaethe Burt O'Dea produces stunning textiles which have featured in *Vogue* magazine. On the premises she makes brilliantly coloured felts by hand – if you're lucky you may see the process – and weaves equally vibrant cloths. The textiles are then made into very desirable and sophisticated garments.

Open: telephone for opening times

BURREN PERFUMERY
Vincent Craft Fragrances, Carron. Tel: (065) 89102

The very last thing you would expect to find in the heart of the Burren's seeming wilderness is a perfumery. Yet, well hidden down a small stony track, Ireland's first perfumery thrives. The oils from plants such as heather, mosses and lichens – all found in abundance in Ireland – are mixed with flowers such as rose or jasmine to make distinctive fragrances.

Although the perfumery is a serious business, it hasn't lost its cottage-industry friendliness. Visitors are made to feel welcome in an informal atmosphere. One of the workers will explain what they are doing – though no one is going to let on the secret of the essence! There is no pressure to buy a scent, though of course you're more than welcome to do so.

Open: May to end Sept, Mon–Sat,
10.00–19.00
Admission free

COUNTY GALWAY

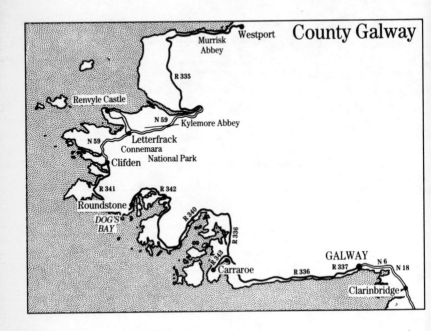

COUNTY GALWAY

Galway is Ireland's second largest county and it offers some breath-taking scenery. Most spectacular of all are perhaps the Twelve Bens, a range of rocky mountains which form a prominent landmark. Across Galway Bay lie the three Aran Islands. These bleak, windswept isles are frequently isolated by the violence of the Atlantic Ocean, which can make crossing by boat impossible. On the islands life is quite different to that of the mainland. The Aran Islands have been settled for thousands of years and on the largest, Inishmore, there survives a massive stone fortress known as Dun Aengus. This impressive pre-historic monument, perched on an exposed 91 m high cliff edge, is said to be one of the finest in Western Europe.

Up until the sixteenth century Ireland was a Gaelic-speaking nation, but from then on the use of the language declined. Initially the decline was due to pressure from the centralized British system of government but it was during the eighteenth century, with the rise of the English-speaking commercial class, that the decline became dramatic. After the famine of the 1840s the decline of spoken Irish Gaelic was severe. The Republic of Ireland is today committed to a policy of Irish Gaelic language revival and Galway is the major centre for An Gaeltacht – the name given to communities throughout Ireland where Irish Gaelic is the spoken language in general use. During June, July and August summer schools are organized throughout Galway. Students stay in the homes of local people and attend classes in the Irish Gaelic language, dancing and music.

DUNGUAIRE CASTLE
Kinvara. Tel: (091) 37108

On the shores of Galway Bay, Dunguaire Castle stands on the site of the seventh-century stronghold of the King of Connaught, Guaire Aidhne. It is from his name, along with the Irish word 'dun', meaning fort, that the castle gets its name. Tradition has it that Guaire Aidhne's right arm grew gradually longer than his left due to his habit of 'giving charitable gold'; he is said to have been known as 'Guaire the Generous'. If you'd like to know more tales and legends associated with the castle take a free guided tour, there're plenty to hear.

Although called a castle, Dunguaire is really a tower house. It is thought that the fashion for tower houses was introduced from Europe and that they became particularly popular in this part of Ireland during the sixteenth century. Typically, a tower house would have been lived in by a gentleman or substantial farmer. This one was built in 1520 and was lived in by a succession of Guaire Aidhne's descendants, the O'Heynes. The position of Dunguaire, between the lands of Connaught to the north and Thomond to the south, and at the foot of the pass at Corker Hill, put it in the direct path of both invading armies. The O'Heynes found it expedient to ally themselves according to the powers of the day.

Today Dunguaire is furnished to give some idea what life in a tower house may have been like right up until its most recent owner left earlier this century. It also offers lovely views over the water to the colourful harbour of Kinvara.

Open: daily, May–Sept,
09.00–17.00
Admission charge

THOOR BALLYLEE – YEATS' TOWER
Gort. Tel: (901) 31436

Admirers of the poetry of William Butler Yeats shouldn't miss the opportunity to take a small excursion inland to see the tower which he

126

made into his summer home. Situated on a bank of a small stream, Thoor Ballylee was once a sixteenth-century tower house built for the De Burgh family. Yeats gradually restored and renovated it, adding a couple of low buildings alongside. On one of its outside walls is the inscription:

> I, the poet William Yeats,
> With old millboards and sea-green slates.
> And smithy work from Gort forge,
> Restored this tower for my wife George.
> And may these characters remain
> When all is ruin once again.

W. B. Yeats was born in Dublin in 1865. He spent much of his early life in Sligo where he studied first painting and then later literature. He acquired Thoor Ballylee after his marriage. It became a retreat for the poet; a place where he could find inspiration. In a letter to Olivia Shakespeare in 1926 he wrote, 'We are at our tower and I am writing poetry as I always do here, and as always happens, no matter how I begin, it becomes love poetry before I am finished with it.' The tower was also a popular place with Yeats' friends who would often stay or visit for dinner. A very helpful tape recording guides visitors through each room in the tower and captures, often using Yeats' own words, its history and its spirit.

Open: May–Sept, 10.00–18.00
Admission charge

CLARINBRIDGE OYSTER FESTIVAL
Clarinbridge

You have to book tickets for the Clarinbridge Oyster Festival well in advance as they are snapped up as soon as they come on sale; locals know a good thing when they see it. The Clarinbridge Oyster Festival is an off-shoot of the better-known Galway Oyster Festival, which takes place a few miles down the road. There is, however, a big difference, very few tourists have discovered Clarinbridge – yet!

All kinds of events such as displays of Irish dancing, fashion shows, art exhibitions, lectures and fancy dress competitions happen during the festival, but the most sought-after tickets are for entry into the festival marquee. A large marquee is pitched beside the river and around midday ticket holders begin to arrive. However, the fun begins much earlier in the adjoining pubs. Jordan's has a great atmosphere, while in Sherry's you may well be invited to sample a delicious bacon-wrapped oyster, on the house.

If you do have a ticket for the marquee be quick to secure a chair on arrival – most of the 800 or so people who pack the tent to the brim have to stand for the entire afternoon. Food is part of the ticket price and it's very good – seafood chowder, oysters (lots of them!) and smoked salmon are usually dished up with fervour if not style. As much lager or stout as you can drink is also part of the deal, so be prepared to stagger out. A tip: although dress is smart, it's a good idea to wear washable garments – as the alcohol begins to flow it also begins to spill. Entertainment is of the home-grown variety, but it doesn't suffer for that. There's an oyster-opening competition and one lucky lad receives the first oyster of the season from a newly-crowned Oyster Queen. All in all the festival makes for a great afternoon's entertainment (and you can expect to do little afterwards!). You're sure to meet many local people and make new friends.

Festival: second week of September

Admission charge: some events are free; for others, including the festival marquee, there is a charge

For dates, full details and programme write well in advance to:
The Secretary, Clarinbridge Oyster Festival, Clarinbridge, Co. Galway

GALWAY
Tourist Information: Eyre Square. Tel: (091) 63081

The history of Galway city dates from medieval times when it was the site of a trading post. A Norman family called De Burgh seized the then small village and around 1240 built a castle. Later in the thirteenth century the family had the surrounding area walled and fortified. In 1484 Richard II of England granted the town a charter of

Killybegs Harbour,
County Donegal
(*The Slide File*)

Patrick Street, Cork
(The Slide File)

Irish Agricultural
Museum, Johnstown
Castle Gardens,
County Wexford
*(Courtesy of The Irish
Agricultural Museum)*

Opposite above: Carrickfergus Castle, County Antrim
(Northern Ireland Tourist Board)

Opposite below: Murlough Bay, County Antrim *(NITB)*

Left: Early sundial at Nendrum Monastic Site, Mahee Island, County Down
(Mary Peplow)

Below: Dunluce Castle, County Antrim *(NITB)*

Above: Dundrum Castle,
County Down
*(© Crown Copyright. Reproduced
with the permission of the Controller of
Her Majesty's Stationery Office)*

Right: Down County
Museum, County Down
(Courtesy of Down Museum)

Opposite above: Annalong
Cornmill, County Down
(NITB)

Opposite below: Tollymore
Forest Park, County Down
(NITB)

Above: Glenariff, County Antrim *(NITB)*

Below: Carrick-a-Rede Rope Bridge, County Antrim *(NITB)*

Mussenden Temple, County Londonderry *(NITB)*

Opposite above: Grey Abbey, County Down *(NITB)*

Opposite below: Mount Stewart Gardens, County Down *(NITB)*

Left: Down Cathedral, Downpatrick, County Down *(Courtesy of Down Museum)*

Below: View of Scrabo Tower across Strangford Lough, County Down *(NITB)*

Above: The National Museum, Dublin *(Bord Fáilte)*

Left: Lissadell House in County Sligo *(Bord Fáilte)*

Above: The Great Hall
in Bunratty Castle,
County Clare *(Courtesy of
Shannon Development)*

Right: Bantry House
overlooking Bantry
Bay, County Cork
(Bord Fáilte)

Above: Entrance to Newgrange passage grave, County Meath *(Bord Fáilte)*

Left: Slieve League Mountain, County Donegal *(Bord Fáilte)*

Below: One of many 'clochans', or Beehive Huts, Dingle Peninsula, County Kerry *(Bord Fáilte)*

Ballyhack Castle, County Wexford *(Bord Fáilte)*

Above: Stephen Pearce Pottery, Shanagarry, County Cork
(Courtesy of Stephen Pearce Pottery)

Below: Avoca Handweavers, Avoca, County Wicklow
(Courtesy of Avoca Handweavers)

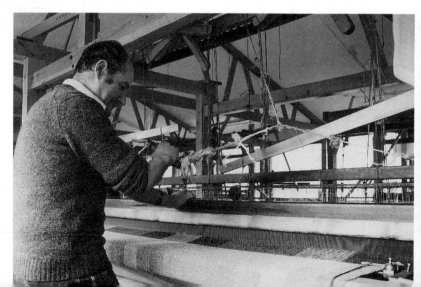

independence to facilitate its flourishing trade with Spain, and in effect created a city-state. Trade with both France and Spain was brisk until the city was taken by Cromwellian forces in 1652 after a nine-month siege. There followed a period of decline, which didn't abate until the eighteenth century when Galway was used by the British government as the administrative centre for the western counties. However, the famine of 1845–8 brought great suffering to Galway, along with the whole of western Ireland, and the Irish economy was depressed. Many people died during the famine and for generations afterwards there was mass emigration to America and Europe.

Today Galway is once again a thriving city. As the capital of western Ireland it is an important commercial centre. It has a university and a growing tourist industry. In addition, Galway is the gateway to Connemara and to the still relatively unspoilt Aran Islands. There are three Aran Islands; the largest is Inishmore, on which stands one of the finest stone fortresses in Europe – Dun Aengus.

Although Galway has a popular seaside suburb known as Salthill, its real charm is its bustling city centre. There are a number of places of interest to visit such as Spanish Arch, Galway City Museum, the Salmon Weir and the Church of St Nicholas (built 1320). All are easily reached on foot, so start a walking tour by dropping into the Tourist Information Office and picking up a street map. However, there's more to be enjoyed in Galway than can be experienced by just 'doing' the tourist trail. Take time to wander into its shops (fresh seafood is a good buy) or linger over a glass of stout in a bar. If you need to stock up on bread or fruit and vegetables, try the street market. Local farmers sell their produce from trestle tables or from the backs of their vans and it's all as fresh as can be. Home-baked bread, cakes and biscuits alongside home-made jams, pickles and delicious farmhouse cheeses are also displayed to tempt shoppers (and they certainly succeed!), while on street corners women with buckets full of eggs call out their wares.

Aran Islands: details of flights and sailings available from the Tourist Information Office

Market: Market Street, Sat, 08.00–14.00

AN CHEATHRU RUA (CARRAROE)

Drive to An Cheathru Rua by car and you will pass through Ros an Mhil (Rossaveal), which retains a number of old thatched cottages grouped in a plan which gives a good idea of life in this kind of settlement in times gone by. Though now a developing fishing harbour, the old part of Ros an Mhil has a special atmosphere. When you reach An Cheathru Rua follow the signposts to Tracoirealach. The road is tiny, hemmed in by higgledy-piggledy stone walls, but persevere because it leads to a small but perfect coral beach. Lapped by turquoise waters over which curlews cry, the beach is said to be unique (not true, but who cares?). Any time of year is a good time to linger on a beautiful coral beach, but autumn is a particularly lovely time. At low tide tresses of seaweed, stranded on pink-grey rocks, glow shades of mustard and burnt orange.

ROUNDSTONE

The village of Roundstone was founded in the mid-1820s by a Scottish engineer, Alexander Nimmo. It was then settled by Scottish fishing people and in 1835 a Franciscan monastery was founded. The site of the monastery has recently been developed for small industry. This has involved the construction of Roundstone Park on the edge of the community. The park is part of a job-creation scheme for rural maritime areas. It contains housing and small industrial units suitable for use as workshops by specialist workers and craftspeople.

Folding Landscapes, Roundstone Harbour. Tel: (095) 35886. Tim Robinson maintains that three of Europe's most fascinating landscapes are grouped around Galway Bay: the Burren (see page 117), the Aran Islands (see page 129) and the bogs and mountains of Connemara. With great skill he has set about mapping their qualities. His most recent project has been to map Connemara in detail – which hasn't been done since 1898 – paying particular attention to Irish place names.

Telephone for opening times

Roundstone Ceramics, Industrial Development Authority (IDA), Roundstone Park. Tel: (095) 35874. The high-fired stoneware and porcelain items at Roundstone Ceramics are all hand-thrown by Seamus Laffin and decorated with coloured slips by Rose O'Toole. Both artists take their inspiration from the local environment: the rugged landscape of Connemara. During the summer they tend to make small pots such as jugs, plates, candle-holders and bowls, mainly for a steadily increasing tourist market, but visit during the winter months and you may catch them producing very individual one-off pieces.

Open: daily, Jan–Nov, 09.30–18.00
Admission free

Roundstone Musical Instruments, IDA Roundstone Park. Tel: (095) 35808. Malachy Kearns makes traditional Irish musical instruments. If you visit his workshop you may see him making anything from tin whistles to harps. The harps are Irish harps, of course, replicas of the Brian Boru harp. They are made from mahogany, beech, birch and Swiss pine and stand 1 m high. More affordable for most visitors is a goatskin bodhran (a musical instrument not unlike a tambourine). The traditional treatment of the goatskin is a craft passed down through generations and it is a well-kept secret. However, Malachy is happy to demonstrate the other processes including how skins are stretched and the rims made. If time allows, children are sometimes offered the chance to stretch a skin over their own tiny bodhran. The finished bodhran may be left plain or it can be hand-painted; Malachy tends to use designs which originated from the Book of Kells (now in Trinity College, Dublin, see page 23), but all sorts of patterns, crests and even insignia can be incorporated.

Open: daily, May–Oct,   **Admission free**
08.00–20.00; Nov–Apr,
09.30–17.00

DOG'S BAY
1.6 km northwest of Roundstone

Dog's Bay is a completely idyllic shore wrapped around with sand dunes and rocks, swept by white sands and sprinkled with shells. Its beauty is breathtaking. There's a narrow peninsula reaching out into the Atlantic Ocean, well colonized by rabbits, which provides a lovely, bracing walk with views over fine white beaches on either side. Incidentally, the name, Dog's Bay, is a corruption of the Irish Gaelic Port na Feadóige, which means Bay of Plovers.

ALCOCK AND BROWN MONUMENT
1.6 km southwest of Clifden

Alcock and Brown were the first people to make a non-stop transatlantic flight. In June 1919 their historic flight ended here in the bogs of Connemara. The monument erected to commemorate their journey is a surprising bomb-shaped limestone construction reached via a narrow roadway through the peat. *Warning*: the kilometre route shouldn't be attempted in any vehicle which doesn't have four-wheel drive; far better to walk and enjoy the scenery.

CLIFDEN

Clifden takes its name from clochan, the Irish word given to an early monastic stone hut built in the shape of a beehive. A clochan once stood on the site in the town now occupied by the Catholic church. The town dates from the nineteenth century and it retains the generously proportioned streets and pretty shop facades of that period. It has developed into a real 'meeting of the roads' with hotels, hostels, restaurants, bars and tourist shops selling all things Celtic.

For a lovely evening walk, take a stroll down by the fishing harbour – it has an unusual view of the village clustering precariously above an inlet of Ardbear Bay. However, for the view to beat all views, take the appropriately named Sky Road. Steeply rising from the west of Clifden, the narrow, precipitous Sky Road climbs high above Clifden Bay, providing a truly breathtaking panorama over some of the many offshore islands of this region.

Clifden is the centre most associated with the Connemara pony. Pony breeding thrives in this area, and during August the town hosts the annual Connemara Pony Show. It's a memorable show which has grown to include exhibitions of all sorts of Irish arts and crafts.

CONNEMARA NATIONAL PARK
Letterfrack. Tel: (095) 41054

The spectacular scenery of Connemara can be daunting to visitors. It can be all too easy to admire the majesty of the mountains from the comfort of a car seat while never venturing into them on foot. Help is at hand; the Connemara National Park is there to tempt even the most lethargic visitor out into the open, as well as doing an important job conserving the landscape.

The park covers some 2,000 hectares of land, including mountains, bogs, heaths, grassland, rivers and a gorge. In the past the land was used for agricultural purposes, cattle grazing mainly, but on the more fertile lowlands some vegetables were grown. These areas are clearly recognizable today along with evidence of human occupation dating back 4,000 years. More recent remains include a nineteenth-century graveyard, a disused lime kiln, old sheep pens and numerous old walls.

A former farm building dating from 1890 has been converted into a visitor centre which offers a number of facilities including an audio-visual introduction to the park, displays, talks, guided walks, information leaflets, good advice and places to picnic both indoors and outdoors. The indoor picnicking provision is a real opportunity for serious mountain walkers to dry out and have a hot meal; the park is exceptionally wet, it has some 250 rainy days each year and an annual rainfall of 1,500 mm. For the less adventurous walker, the park has two nature trails. Along each the aspects of the Connemara scenery are explained. For instance, you can learn about so-called lazy-beds. These are cultivation ridges cut either by spade or with a plough. They were dug to provide land for cultivation. The size of the ridges depended on the type of soil and on the crop. The nature trails also give information about the area's vegetation and wildlife. There are numerous heathers to spot, including ling and bell heather, and in the blanket bog there's an abundance of purple moor-grass, bog moss, bog cotton and bog rush. One popular trail feature is the pony paddock where a herd of pure-bred Connemara ponies attract lots of attention.

Open: daily, May–Sept,   **Admission charge** (car park only)
10.00–18.30

Talks and guided walks during July
and August only

KYLEMORE ABBEY
Nr Letterfrack

The castellated mansion of Kylemore Abbey has the sort of picturesque setting which makes coach parties stop to take snapshots. Viewed first across the still waters of a lake, and with the Dorruagh mountains rising almost perpendicularly behind, the abbey seems to fit perfectly into its setting. Sadly, however, Kylemore is no longer an abbey; it has been converted into a girls' school. Only the hall and the library are open to the public, but it's well worth wandering through the grounds to take a look at the small Gothic chapel, which is richly decorated with Connemara marble.

The lake in front of the abbey is one of three which form Kylemore Abbey Fishery. They are all kept well stocked with salmon and sea trout.

Open: daily, mid-March to Oct,
09.00–18.30
Admission free

At the end of a promontory, all that remains of fourteenth-century Renvyle Castle, once a stronghold of the O'Flahertys, is a crumbling facade. Still, it's no less dramatic for that, and the extensive beach with views out to small islands where white horses break continuously makes it worth the drive. In addition, the route from Connemara National Park to Renvyle does pass through some pretty scenery, including the village of Tully Cross. Here you can see some traditional Irish thatched cottages, all sprucely painted in reds and greens (in fact they are newly renovated holiday cottages, which can be rented by visitors). Renvyle House Hotel is worth a thought; it was the summer home of writer-physician Oliver St John Gogarty, who was a contemporary of James Joyce and the character Mulligan in *Ulysses*. The castle is not open to the public, but can be easily viewed from the road.

COUNTY MAYO

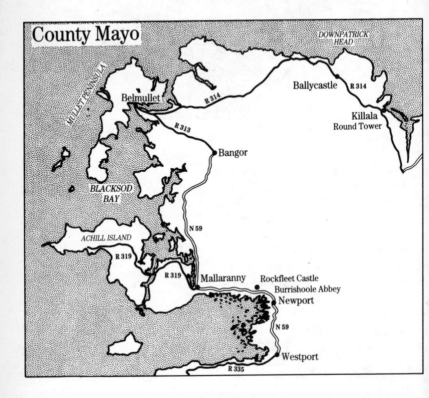

COUNTY MAYO

Mayo's coastline is long and unspoilt. It stretches from Killary Harbour on the edge of Connemara in the south, to Killala Bay in the north. Wild, beautiful and silent are the words which seem to sum it up best. That's not to say it doesn't have plenty of life, towns such as Westport are both lively and colourful, but it is desolate windswept vistas which predominate. In some parts the land is very sparsely populated, those in search of solitude can find it here amidst silent bogs where the only sounds are those of the wind and the seabirds. However, nowhere is completely deserted. In even the most isolated parts an unexpected cottage signals human habitation.

Prehistoric people settled in the Mayo region around 3000 BC. Evidence of their presence can be seen particularly in the bogland of the northwest where many court-tombs have survived. Mayo's recorded history begins in the seventh century when it was settled by English monks who founded a major monastery. The place was known as Maigh Eo na Sacsan meaning 'the plain of the yew trees of the English', and hence the name Mayo. The land was ruled by powerful Irish families until the twelfth century when it was invaded by the Normans, who are said to have gradually become 'more Irish than the Irish'. Certainly some of the commonest names in Mayo today, such as Joyce and Burke, are Norman in origin. In the sixteenth century the English monarchy made a forceful attempt to control Mayo which was opposed by the now legendary Grace O'Malley. She became a sea captain and is even said to have visited Queen Elizabeth I in London. However, English forces gained firm control over the area and from 1600 it was under English administration. When Cromwell's army took the east of Ireland in the mid-seventeenth century, the Irish there were dispossessed of their fertile land and sent to 'to hell or Connaught'. Many arrived in Mayo to eke out an existence. The blighted potato crops between 1845 and 1847 brought widespread famine to Mayo, as they did to the rest of Ireland. James Daly wrote, '200,000 died of hunger in Mayo, after living on nettles and asses flesh.' In places the population was halved and the decline continued until around 1960.

Bleak, yet lovely, the Mayo coast has a particular quality which perhaps takes a little longer to absorb than the immediate grandeur of the Galway region. Nevertheless, it's worth persevering because the forbidding quality eventually gives way to a quiet tranquillity.

MURRISK ABBEY
8 km west of Westport

Founded in 1457 by an Augustinian order, Murrisk Abbey was built on lands donated by Teigh O'Malley, chieftain of the O'Malley Clan. It was closely associated with the nearby mountain, Croagh Patrick, where St Patrick, Ireland's patron saint, is said to have prayed and fasted for forty days and forty nights. The abbey is also said to have housed relics of the saint – St Patrick's tooth (Fiacail Padhraic) and the Black Bell of St Patrick (Clog Dubh) – which are now in the National Museum, Dublin. It is a local tradition that St Patrick quelled the strength of the Celtic god Crom Dubh and cast him and his demons into a hole at the foot of the mountain called Lug-na-nDeamhan (Hollow of Demons). It is also said that Patrick stood on the south side of the mountain, where there's a steep drop, and rang his bell. On hearing its chimes all the snakes of Ireland are said to have come up the mountain and hurled themselves over the precipice and thus Ireland was rid of snakes for ever!

In 1577 the Augustinians were driven from their lands as a consequence of the Protestant Reformation. However, they remained in the area and it is thought that by 1635 they were once more installed in the abbey. The main evidence for this is that two inscribed chalices exist. One is marked, 'Pray for Theobald Lord Viscount Mayo and his wife Maeve Ni Cnochoure, who had me made for the Monastery in the Year of the Lord 1635.' The other bears the words, 'Friar John de Burgo Augustinian, caused me to be made for the house of Murrisk in the year 1648.'

The picturesque ruins which survive have a beautiful setting on the shores of the bay. When the tide is out the mud flats and seaweed create a reflective panorama which reads like an abstract painting and the distant mountains provide a delicate frame.

Open: all the time
Admission free

WESTPORT HOUSE
Westport. Tel: (098) 25194

Many legends surround the dungeons of Westport House, which have been developed into a blood-curdling chamber of horrors – children love it. The dungeons belonged to an ancient castle, owned by the O'Malleys, which once stood on this site. That was at a time before the dam was constructed and the sea still washed the walls of the castle at high tide. The building which can be seen today is of a very different sort and it is set into a very different landscape. Westport House is a Georgian mansion situated beside a peaceful lake with views over Clew Bay.

The original house was built for Colonel John Browne, an ancestor of the present Marquess of Sligo. It was subsequently adapted first by German architect Robert Cassels and then by English architect James Wyatt. In 1730 Cassels designed the east front, which was made by local craftsmen using limestone from the nearby quarry. Wyatt was responsible for the south face, which dates from 1778. The work of both architects can be seen inside the house.

The front hall is the first room visitors see and it has a fine barrel ceiling by Cassels. It may look a little grubby, but that's not surprising because it retains its original Georgian paint. To the left of the hall there's a comfortable library filled with leather-bound books. The library is also the home of 'Pinky', a most unusual house guest. This six-foot-tall bright pink rabbit is a genial host, although he does sometimes greet visitors at unexpected moments.

The oak staircase, which is topped by a stunning ceiling and lit by a lovely stained-glass window, and the pretty morning room were designed by Wyatt, while the white Sicilian marble staircase is the work of Italian craftsmen. Upstairs, one of the most interesting rooms is the Chinese room. It is covered with delicate 200-year-old Chinese wallpaper.

Out in the grounds there's an amusement arcade, a children's zoo and a host of other activities, including pony riding and tennis.

Open: daily, mid-May to mid-Sept,
14.00–18.00
Admission charge

WESTPORT
Westport Tourist Office, The Mall. Tel: (098) 25711

Westport must rate as one of the most attractive of all Irish towns. Well organized with a pleasing sense of proportion and scale, the town was obviously carefully designed, but by whom no one is quite sure. Locals will happily tell you it is the work of this or that architect; there's a tale that it was laid out by a French architect left behind after Humbert's expedition of 1798; others think it was designed by James Wyatt. Whoever was responsible, they did a good job. The town's central feature is the Octagon, around which buildings are angled, their order broken in three places by radiating streets. The streets themselves have retained a great deal of original detail and there's a mall lined with lime trees running alongside the River Carrowbeg. The river itself has been canalized and it is still spanned by an eighteenth-century bridge.

Westport positively buzzes with activity. Cars pack the space around the Octagon, pavements are full of people going about their business and shops are well stocked and inviting. The town doesn't go to sleep at night either as it boasts a number of restaurants, bars and, during the summer, discotheques. Westport becomes most crowded (though never too full) at festival time. There are three annual festivals: Sea Angling (June); Athletics (August); Arts (October).

However, most visitors tend to stroll around the streets, do a little shopping and then go on to explore the beaches or take a look at the quayside.

Details of festivals from the
Tourist Information Office

NEWPORT

No one would describe Newport as a picture-postcard-pretty town, but it does have character and it's worth taking a look. There's a short walk leading down to the harbour which Thackeray described as 'a miracle of beauty'. Well, maybe . . . but that was a long time ago. Still, the view across the river remains attractive enough to make the stroll pleasant.

The town's main charm is generated by the old railway bridge whose seven arches span the Brown Oak River. The town itself stretches up a steep hill which is lined with shops (with barely a tourist trinket in sight) and several rather ugly churches. Newport is mainly known as a fishing resort – both at sea and in the nearby loughs, Beltra, Furnace and Feeagh. However, there are other things to do including visiting the remnants of a cottage once lived in by Princess Grace of Monaco.

BURRISHOOLE ABBEY
Nr Newport

The remains of Burrishoole Abbey, just a short way from the town of Newport, are picturesquely sited on the water's edge. In the autumn you may see a farmer harvesting the seaweed to spread on the land in the time-honoured way. The ruins are very well maintained, there are tidy gravel pathways throughout, and the graves are neatly set into lawns. Nevertheless, you're unlikely to see many fellow visitors at this out of the way haven.

The abbey was founded by a Dominican order in the fifteenth century. Of the walls and buildings still standing the solid central tower is best preserved along with its vault, which is supported by Romanesque arches. The rest of the abbey is crumbling away, but it provides a tranquil spot to sit for a while and contemplate the lovely island-dotted sweep of Clew Bay.

Open: daily
Admission free

CARRIGHOOLEY CASTLE (Rockfleet Castle)
Nr Newport

Many ruined castles and towers in this area claim to be associated with the so-called 'Pirate Queen', Grace O'Malley (Grainne Uaile). Carrighooley, however, has the distinction of being positively documented as one of her strongholds. It was from here that she beat off an English attack in 1574.

Grace O'Malley was the daughter of the Chief of the Western Islands, Owen O'Malley. When her father died, Grace made herself ruler of the lands around Clew Bay. Her exploits at sea earned her the tag 'Pirate Queen', while her feats of war earned her the name 'Grainne of Heroes'. Many legends surround her life, but perhaps one of the most fascinating is associated with her wedding contract. Tradition has it that the contract she made with her second husband, Mac-William Oughter, contained an unusual clause. The couple agreed that after a year of marriage either partner could break the contract by saying to the other 'I dismiss you'. During that first year of marriage Grace garrisoned all MacWilliam's castles with her own followers. At the end of the period, as MacWilliam was entering Carrighooley Castle, Grace called to him from inside, 'I dismiss you.' Thus she is said to have gained MacWilliam's strongholds.

Carrighooley today is a peaceful place to visit. Its simple tower washed gently by the waters from the bay commands a delightful vista over a long stretch of water to the open sea beyond.

Open: daily, 10.00–18.00 (key with
caretaker)
Admission free

ACHILL ISLAND

You reach Achill Island by crossing a short bridge from the mainland. At 24 km long and 19 km across, Achill is the largest island off the Irish coast. Great tracts of its land are swathed in heather and bog which together create a strange anonymity. However, the presence of three high mountains provides a sense of drama. The highest, at 672 m, is Slievemore, then comes Croghaun at 668 m and finally Minaun at 466 m. From the foot of Minaun curves a sandy beach two miles long which has become a popular family attraction. In recent years the resort of Keel has developed along the shore. Small-scale whitewashed cottages speckle the surrounding barren grandeur making Keel look like a toy village. Just as a miniature golf course is dotted with funny buildings to amuse children, Keel is dotted with restaurants, hotels and gift shops to amuse tourists.

Tourism, particularly fishing, has offered a lifeline to an island whose inhabitants for centuries barely subsisted; many families relied on money sent home from relatives living abroad. A poignant reminder of the hardship they suffered is the sight of the ruined buildings and scattered graves at Doogort and Missionary Settlement. It was here, in 1830, that one Reverend Edward Nangle of the Church Missionary Society used the islanders' poverty to attempt to stop them speaking their own language and to convert them to the English church. He founded a church and a school, and only children who attended were fed and clothed by the mission. During a time of terrible poverty when many were starving the scheme attracted many desperate youngsters. It was praised by such eminent people as Thomas Carlyle, who personally visited it. However, other more thoughtful contemporary visitors, Mr and Mrs Hall, remarked that, 'The divine precept that teaches forgiveness . . . had not been learned if it was taught in the colony.' The couple were, however, enchanted with the island and commented on its wild beauty.

It is an essentially untamed beauty which can be enjoyed today. Achill Sound, though small, is the island's main shopping centre. From here an aptly named Atlantic Drive is signposted. It's worth following this route to take in some spectacular coastal scenery including a fine view over Ashleam Bay. You may even be lucky and spot a rare bird – a few golden eagles survive here. The drive also passes through Kildownet where a tower associated with Grace O'Malley (see Carrighooley Castle, p. 144) stands and nearby there's a small ruined twelfth-century church.

THE MULLET PENINSULA

Leaving Achill take the long windswept road to Bangor. Mesmerizing miles of bog stretch out on either side, but in the spring a ribbon of gaudy colour is created by flowering wild rhododendrons which line parts of the route. From Bangor take the road out towards Belmullet.

Belmullet, at the north tip of Blacksod Bay, is the major settlement on the peninsula. From here you can hire boats, join organized fishing trips, or simply explore the area. Despite its wild environment, the peninsula has a long history of habitation dating from prehistoric times. Remains from more recent times can still be seen. Perched on a cliff top are the ruins of Doonamo fort (8 km northwest from Belmullet), a walled promontory defence built by early settlers. More ruins can be seen at Cross Abbey (8 km southwest of Belmullet), a medieval priory church built on the very edge of the sea. Cross is said to have associations with St Brendan, the sixth-century sea voyager. Legends connected to The Mullet abound including the story of the children of Lir. Having been turned into swans by their wicked stepmother, the four children of Lir are said to have spent 300 years on the tiny island of Inishglora (1½ km off The Mullet coast). On the island a small twelfth-century chapel dedicated to St Brendan survives; it's entirely built of drystone masonry.

Many visitors to The Mullet are keen ornithologists. There are plenty of birds to be seen, including teal, shelduck, and brent and Greenland white-fronted geese. It is also the only nesting place in Ireland of the great phalarope.

DOWN PATRICK HEAD
Nr Ballycastle

The short walk to the top of this headland is well worth the effort to get a good view of the dramatic ragged cliffs over which the sea seems to splinter like trillions of crushed glacier mints. Constant pounding by the waves has created many blow-holes up through which the sea roars. A large wedge-shaped rock has broken away entirely and it's only a matter of time before more of the headland is snatched by the powerful water.

Walking up to the headland you'll pass over an ancient circular settlement together with a memorial to local people who lost their lives in the aftermath of the rebellion of 1798. The memorial stands beside a deep hole at the bottom of which the sea pounds remorselessly. It was down this hole that those villagers who had joined the rebellion were flung to their deaths.

RATHFRAN ABBEY
Off R314, Nr Killala

As with so many of Ireland's abbeys, Rathfran Abbey is situated on the banks of a gentle inlet surrounded by beautiful land. Though now much ruined, the shape of this Dominican establishment can be more clearly seen than most, including a whole complex of rooms which can be 'read' in plan.

A good reason to visit the abbey is to take a stroll up the lane past the churchyard and down a small farm track (always very muddy) to a secluded beach where curlews call. When the tide is out the bay is one huge bowl of wet golden sand.

Sharp eyes will spot numerous ancient sites near the abbey, including the Breastagh Ogham Stone. This single standing stone is thought to date from the Bronze Age – it is inscribed with writing that dates from between 300 and 600 AD.

Open: all the time
Admission free

Killala is a fairly ordinary small town today, and its main claim to fame is that its bishopric is believed to have been founded by St Patrick. However, its most striking feature must be the round tower which rises above a cluster of small houses and shops like a pointing index finger. Tradition has it that the tower was originally a lighthouse, but in fact it was most likely a belfry. It was also probably a place of security – the entrance is via a door some 4 m from the ground. Built of limestone, the tower is 26 m high and is thought to be the work of a travelling group of builders who moved around the country constructing a series of similar buildings.

Open: daily (key with caretaker next door)
Admission free

COUNTY SLIGO

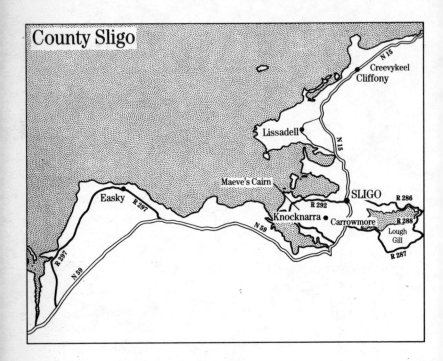

COUNTY SLIGO

For its small size, County Sligo has a relatively long stretch of coastline which wraps around Sligo Bay. The Ox Mountains form a majestic and timeless backdrop to the first part of the coastal route. They contain rock dating back some six hundred million years. The coastline itself is mainly low-lying and fringed by lovely sandy beaches. Sligo's beauty has been immortalized by writer W. B. Yeats, winner of a Nobel Prize, who described it as 'land of heart's desire', and by his artist brother, J. B. Yeats. The Yeats family spent many summers in Sligo and W. B. Yeats is now buried in Drumcliff churchyard.

Like much of the west coast of Ireland, County Sligo is sparsely populated and its empty roads are a joy to travel. With the exception, that is, of the town of Sligo, which bustles with activity, particularly on market day.

The county has a great number of archaeological sites, many of good quality. Remains of Mesolithic hunters and gatherers have been found as well as burial tombs of four later groups of people. These were early farmers and they have been named after the stone tombs they built – the Court Tomb People, the Portal Tomb People, the Passage Tomb People, and the Wedge Tomb People. Ring forts and stone forts characteristic of early Celts can be seen, as well as hill forts belonging to later chieftains and local kings. Ireland, never conquered by the Romans, presents a classic opportunity to study the Celts and prehistory, and County Sligo is particularly rich in remains, though no one as yet knows for sure why it was such a popular place for early settlements.

This is a potentially pretty town, but the greyness of the buildings at its centre tends to deaden the imagination of anyone seeking the picturesque. However, the Easky River adds a lively note and the ruins of Roslee Castle at its mouth are something for the energetic to clamber over. A stranger sight is 'Split Rock'. It's easy to miss so ask for the village school and you'll find this peculiar phenomenon directly opposite.

'Split Rock' is in fact a glacial erratic which took its current form during the Ice Age. As its name suggests, it split down its centre. Local people have an explanation for their unusual monument, which they call 'Fionn MacCool's Finger'. Fionn, the tale goes, tried to throw the stone into the sea from the top of the Ox Mountains as a wager. As the mountains are some 22½ km away it isn't surprising that he lost his bet. However, the stone is said to have landed just 1 km short and in anger Fionn struck it, causing it to split in two. Local legend says that it will close up on anyone who dares to go through the split three times . . .

Roslee Castle
Open: all the time
Admission free

MISCAUN MEADHBH (MAEVE'S CAIRN)
Knocknarra, Nr Carrowmore

It takes about 45 minutes to climb up to the top of Knocknarra following a path which is hemmed in on both sides by drystone walls. Do choose a clear day for your trek up Knocknarra, which Yeats described as a 'cairn-heaped grassy hill', because the views from its summit are spectacular. Slieve League and Donegal can be seen to the north while the Ox Mountains and Croagh Patrick are to the south-west. There's also a fine view over Sligo Bay, which glints temptingly in the sunshine. Choose a misty day for your walk and you'll have an altogether different experience. When clouds shroud the landscape, the deserted hilltop becomes an eerie world from which Maeve's Cairn looms menacingly. Traditionally, this 24 m cairn is believed to have been built for Queen Maeve of Rathcroghan, who reigned in the first century AD (she was the 'Queen Mab' of English folktales). Experts now think it was built by Stone Age farmers around 3000 BC.

Open: all the time
Admission free

HOLY WELL
Nr Lough Gill

Holy Well is a religious shrine dedicated to the Virgin Mary. It's an enchanting spot, in a woody glen near the banks of Lough Gill, which offers peace to all who visit. A pretty stream runs through a small grotto, which also contains, as its name suggests, a Holy Well. Amongst the trees and ferns there are graves and votive statues while set into moss-covered rock there's a small altar.

Open: all the time
Admission free

SLIGO
Tourist information: Temple Street. Tel: (071) 61201

Sunday is a peaceful day in Sligo, the shops are closed and people are either with their families or at church, but every other day is chaotic and noisy. Here you are likely to experience your first major traffic jam on the west coast. Sligo vibrates with the sound of lorries as they criss-cross the city on their way to other major cities in the north, south and east. Cars form long tail-backs queueing to get into car parks. However, if you need to do some basic shopping this is the place to make for. Sligo, as the county town, has numerous shops stocking everything you might need, except perhaps touristy knickknacks. When you've done your shopping you might like to explore the city, it has more than just stores to offer the visitor.

The first known mention of Sligo was in 807 AD when it was sacked by the Vikings. It started to expand during the thirteenth century when, after the Norman invasion, it was granted to Maurice Fitzgerald, who built himself a castle at the west end of today's Castle Street. No remains survive of this early castle nor of a later Cromwellian one. The only ancient building to survive in Sligo is the abbey, built during medieval times. There are, however, a great deal of eighteenth- and nineteenth-century buildings which were certainly to the taste of Thomas Carlyle who wrote, 'Sligo at last; beautiful descent into beautiful town.'

A useful tourist trail booklet can be obtained from the tourist information office. It guides you on a walking tour of Sligo city taking in some of its most interesting sights. It may take some imagination to conjure up pictures of a medieval settlement, but with the help of this handy booklet you won't miss any of the city's more recent architectural treasures.

Sligo has one major claim to fame, its unique relationship with the Yeats family:

Municipal Art Gallery, St Stephens Street. Tel: (071) 42212. The Municipal Art Gallery, attached to the County Library, houses a surprisingly good collection of paintings by Irish artists and in particular many works by Jack B. Yeats, including oils, watercolours and drawings.

Open: Mon–Fri, 10.30–12.30 and
14.30–16.30
Admission free

Sligo Art Gallery, Yeats Memorial Building, Hyde Bridge. Tel: (071) 45847. Here, in the headquarters of the Yeats International Summer School, lectures are given by recognized authorities on Yeats and his contemporaries in the Irish literary movement. In the gallery temporary exhibitions are held regularly throughout the year.

Open: during exhibitions, **Admission free**
Mon–Fri, 10.00–14.00 and
15.00–17.00; Sat, 10.00–13.00

LISSADELL HOUSE
Lissadell. Tel: (071) 63150

Visits to Lissadell House are by guided tour only. This is the ancestral home of the Gore-Booth family, and each tour is led by a member of the family. It is the personal quality of the tour, with every photograph and painting being carefully explained, which makes each visitor feel like an invited guest. Comfortable rooms are filled with objects collected by the family over generations; an imposing hall tells of large parties and musical evenings. Lissadell House is today cold and somewhat threadbare with the faded elegance of a country house which belongs to another era and yet its magic hasn't completely dissolved. At the end of the afternoon it isn't too difficult to see the house through the eyes of W. B. Yeats:

> The light of the evening at Lissadell,
> Great windows open to the south,
> Two girls in silk kimonos, both
> Beautiful, one gazelle.
> But a raving autumn shears
> Blossom from summer's wreath;
> The older is condemned to death,
> Pardoned drags out lonely years
> Conspiring among the ignorant.
> I know not what the younger dreams –
> Some vague Utopia – and she seems,
> When withered old and skeleton-gaunt,
> An image of such politics
> Many time I think to seek
> One or the other out and speak
> Of that old Georgian mansion, mix
> Pictures of the mind, recall
> That table and the talk of youth,
> Two girls in silk kimonos, both
> Beautiful, one gazelle.

The poem is written in memory of Eva Gore-Booth and her sister, Constance. Constance, Countess Markievicz, was a leader in the 1916 uprising. She was sentenced to death and then reprieved. Two years later she was elected as a Member of Parliament in the British House of Commons, though she never took her seat. She was also a member of the first Dail. Yeats was a regular visitor to Lissadell and is now buried in nearby Drumcliff churchyard.

Constance's activities and the association with Yeats tends to overshadow the history of Lissadell. However, apart from a few mementos and a windowpane scratched with Constance's signature, there is little to be seen of these two famous people. What haunts the visitor's mind instead is a sense of decay, of a time now passed, and a certain poignant beauty.

Open: 1 May to end Sept
Admission charge

CREEVYKEEL COURT CAIRN
Nr Cliffony on N15

Cars and lorries pass by Creevykeel Court Cairn daily, their occupants little realizing that one of the finest examples in Ireland of a court cairn is situated just beside the highway. Creevykeel is a large, enclosed, open-air court which dates back over 3,000 years. The remains are very clear and well preserved. Because of its shape experts believe that rituals may have been carried out within the complex before the dead were buried in the covered tomb at the back of the court. It's also thought that during the early Christian period the central part of the cairn was used for iron smelting.

Open: all the time
Admission free

COUNTY DONEGAL

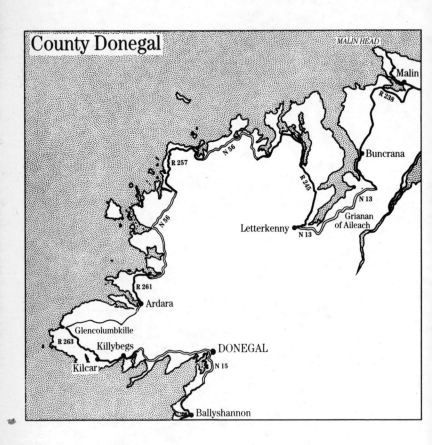

COUNTY DONEGAL

Donegal is the most northerly county in the Republic of Ireland. Its coastline is an extremely wild and rugged landscape, its spectacular exposed cliffs are pounded by an untamed ocean. Yet there are secluded beaches, refuges from the wind and fierce water, where you can enjoy gentle walks on golden sands.

The further north you travel the wilder the scenery becomes. Moors and mountains are only occasionally dotted with sturdy dwellings, and small villages huddle in sheltered harbours. Here, to the north of Killybegs, Irish Gaelic is the spoken language, though most of the people speak English as a second language. County Donegal contains the largest native Irish Gaelic speaking population of any Irish county, and the people are keen to preserve their cultural and linguistic traditions.

Donegal has been settled for over 7,000 years. Recent archaeological finds show that inlets in the north of the county were used all those thousands of years ago by hunting and fishing people who are thought to have moved camp regularly to take advantage of varying seasonal resources. Later, during the Neolithic and early Bronze Ages, early farmers raised livestock in the same region. Their tombs have been found in abundance. Agriculture continued to develop and there is evidence that the bog which now blankets large tracts of land was once fertile arable land which was sectioned off into fields. On the coast numerous ancient middens have been found.

Today Donegal is known for its breathtaking scenery and for its tweed which reflects the wonderful colours of the region.

DONEGAL CRAFT VILLAGE
Ballyshannon Road

With the revival of traditional cottage crafts, due mainly to the demand created by tourism, a number of centres such as Donegal Craft Village have been created. The 'village' is a group of purpose-built units grouped around a common courtyard. Each unit houses a craftworker whose talent might be weaving, painting, jewellery-making or pottery. There's also a furniture maker, a batik artist, a metal worker and, perhaps more unusually, a fibre artist. However, craftworkers do leave from time to time and are replaced by others who may have a different talent so it's impossible to say for sure what's being produced within the village at any one time – it's best to go and have a look for yourself.

Open: May–Sept, Mon–Sat,
10.00–18.00
Admission free

DONEGAL

Weaving is the activity for which Donegal and the surrounding region is chiefly known; its tradition is so old that there's no verifiable start to its development. It's always been a hereditary skill, passed from generation to generation. Originally crofters' wives made vats of colour from moss and lichen found locally. The new wool from the household's sheep was dipped into it and dyed. Husbands would then weave long stretches of cloth which were later sold at market in the town of Donegal.

Today Donegal is still the centre of the weaving industry and not surprisingly it specializes in woven fabrics which reflect the lovely colours of the surrounding countryside. Many shops in Donegal sell hand-woven pieces of fabric and a wide variety of goods made from it such as scarves, jackets, rugs and shawls. In the window of Magee's on the main road you may even see, during the summer months, a master weaver at work using a wooden handloom. These looms differ only slightly from those used in biblical times. Weaving of complicated designs in complex permutations of colour is a highly skilled process, but the weavers accomplish it with seemingly effortless speed.

Most of the weaving shops are situated around what is known as the Diamond, the town's central square. The Diamond makes a good starting point for a tour of the town; for a small charge you can pick up locally a handy guide to a walking tour of Donegal ('A Signposted Walking Tour of Donegal Town'). Perhaps the most picturesque of the buildings of historic interest described in the guide is Donegal Friary. It's often wrongly thought to be an abbey, but is in fact a Franciscan house dating from around 1474. Successive raids over the centuries have reduced the friary to ruins, but it's worth a look nonetheless. Look out too for the 4.6 m long anchor which you'll pass on the quayside as you walk towards the friary. It has links with Napoleon, Wolfe Tone and the rebellion of 1798.

KILLYBEGS

Killybegs is one of Ireland's most important fishing centres, as your nose will immediately tell you as you enter the town. The whole place reeks with the smell of fish. Trawlers from many European ports come to dock here, making for a crowded and colourful harbour. When the fishing fleet is in, the quayside is a hive of activity and noise. Seagulls circle overhead, keen to take their share of the catch. Most of the haul is, however, destined for human palates and is quickly bought for restaurants throughout Ireland as well as for domestic cooking.

Although Killybegs was granted borough status in 1616 by King James, its appearance today is essentially Victorian. Its most impressive building is St Catherine's Church, which was built in 1840 to the designs of J. B. Papworth. Note the image of a gallowglass on the tombstone of one Niall Mor MacSuibhne; it's near the tower. Gallowglasses were medieval mercenary soldiers from Scotland who were hired by leading Irish and Anglo-Irish families of whom the MacSuibhnes were the most notable.

STUDIO DONEGAL
Kilcar. Tel: (073) 38002

Kilcar is a major centre for handloom weaving and as you might expect there are numerous shops selling goods made from the cloth. At Studio Donegal you can see local handloom weavers at work. In a room above the shop, weavers' looms clack all day long producing fabric the colour of the surrounding mountains. The goods produced include a complete range of coats and suits along with more affordable small items such as tea cosies made from off-cut scraps.

Open: Mon–Fri, 9.00–17.00
Admission free

FOLK VILLAGE MUSEUM
Glencolumbkille. Tel: (073) 30017

The folk village is small, just a handful of cottages, but represents an effort on behalf of the local community, many of whom have contributed to the contents. The cottages are fairly recent constructions, which unfortunately have not been furnished with historical accuracy, but there's still plenty of interest to see and learn. Visits are by guided tour only. The tours are entertaining and will fill you in on all sorts of bits of information. For instance, in one of the cottages there's a chair which is said to have been made from wood washed ashore from the Spanish Armada which was wrecked some 400 years ago. Rafters for the cottages, which have been constructed in the traditional way, are even older. The wood to make the rafters was gathered from the surrounding bog where it had been preserved for 4,000 years. As you travel through the area you'll notice stumps of wood sticking out of the bog; the chances are that these too are many thousands of years old.

Open: Easter to end Apr, Mon–Fri, 10.00–18.00; May to end Aug, daily, 10.00–20.00; Sept, daily, 10.00–18.00   **Admission free**

GRIANAN OF AILEACH
Off Letterkenny/Buncrana road

Little is known of this fine circular stone fort which is thought to date from early Christian times. However, if not for its historic significance then for its beauty and setting Grianan of Aileach is worth searching out. Its well-restored walls enclose an area 23 m in diameter, and are 4 m thick. At intervals stone steps lead up to a walkway round its perimeter. There are wonderful views over the Foyle valley, the Atlantic coast and the brooding mountains of Donegal.

Open: all the time
Admission free

MALIN, MALIN HEAD

Anyone who listens to the radio will be familiar with the shipping forecasts and with the rough weather which frequently visits this part of the coast. Malin Head is the most northerly point in Ireland, a spot worth going to if only to say you've been! There's little to see or do here except contemplate the power of the sea.

The village of Malin is, however, interesting. It's a well-preserved seventeenth-century 'plantation' town (see p. 167); indeed it's even retained its original triangular village green. One end of the green is dominated by the parish church with its surprising three-stage battlemented tower and square pinnacles.

COUNTY
LONDONDERRY

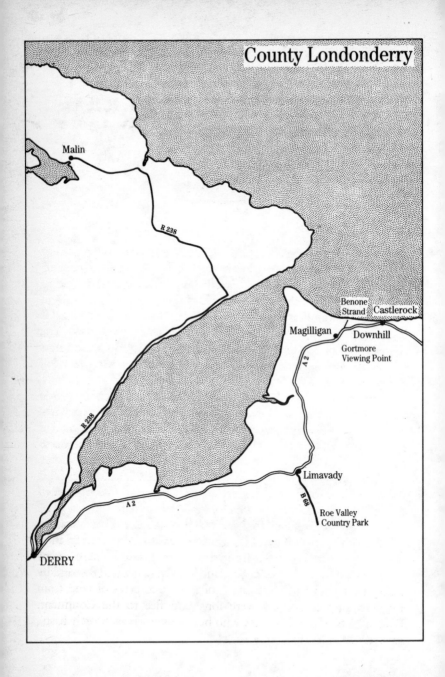

County Londonderry

COUNTY LONDONDERRY

The name Londonderry was officially given to the area by James I of England in a charter. It's a lovely region containing long uninterrupted beaches and splendid mountains. Its coastal landscape is, however, significantly softer than neighbouring Atlantic-swept Donegal. Londonderry is part of Northern Ireland while Donegal is in the Republic of Ireland; you pass through a border crossing. The coastline of Londonderry is mainly washed by the more gentle waters of Lough Foyle, which forms a deep bay with the county town of Derry at its head.

Derry is said to have been founded in the sixth century by St Colmcille who built a monastery here. Tradition has it that when Colmcille was given the land on which to build a monastery by Aid mac Ainmire, the first thing he did was to set fire to it. His aim was to purify the land of all its previous history. However, the fire was so fierce that it nearly destroyed the nearby oak forest. St Colmcille is said to have prayed for the fire to stop, which it duly did. The Irish word for oak is daire, and it is this which gives Derry its name.

The surrounding area contains many plantation towns, such as seventeenth-century Limavady, which are easily recognized by their wide main streets and flat-fronted terraced houses. These towns were formed by settlers from Scotland who were granted the land by James I after he had confiscated some 750,000 acres of land from Ireland's aristocracy who were forced to flee to the Continent. Descendants of the 'Planters', who became known as 'Scotch-Irish', later settled in North America.

Derry straddles the River Foyle not far from where it flows into Lough Foyle. It is Northern Ireland's second city, and is a place rarely out of the news for long. 'The troubles' have left the place scarred – barbed wire, road-blocks, the occasional bombed-out building, derelict houses and plenty of graffiti. And yet . . . A favourite word used by those who wish to promote a positive view of Derry is 'potential'; the city has great potential. At its heart there is a busy shopping centre which radiates from the Diamond, the square which is part of the original medieval street plan. Lovely terraces of Georgian buildings are also plentiful. Small side streets offer unexpectedly interesting views. Nevertheless, while for the inhabitants of Derry road-blocks and armed police are a fact of everyday life, for the visitor they are an unnerving anathema. But whatever Derry's present problems, it remains a city worth visiting.

Amelia Earhart Cottage, off Culmore Road. Tel: (0504) 53379. Amelia Earhart was the first woman to fly solo across the Atlantic. Her historic flight is commemorated by a cottage which has been built near to the field in which she landed on 21 May 1932. The cottage contains a small exhibition connected to her flight together with information about natural history.

Open: Tues–Sat, 10.00–16.00
Admission free

City Walls Derry is known as the maiden city because its great surrounding walls, which date from 1618, are the most nearly complete walls to be seen anywhere in the British Isles. They include seven arch gates (four original, three later insertions), six bastions and many cannons. Until recent times you could walk their one-mile route and have panoramic views over the city. Sadly, considered by the police a security risk, the walkway is now mostly closed to the public.

St Columb's Cathedral, St Columb, founder of the monastery on Iona, was born in 521 AD into a noble family. He has been described as 'a prince by birth, a priest by choice, and a saint by grace'. St Columb's Cathedral, built in the seventeenth century, retains much of its original shape. It is built in a style which has become known as 'Planters Gothic'. When it was being constructed there were only 155 families living in Derry; by the time it was completed the town had become an important centre.

Open: Mon–Sat
Admission free

ROE VALLEY COUNTRY PARK
Off B192. Tel: (05047) 62074

Many people are attracted to Roe Valley Country Park for its outdoor activities such as canoeing, but there are plenty of less energetic things to do too. Most popular are the riverside walks, which pass through pretty woodlands. The river is an important feature as it was once a major source of power; a hydro-electric plant harnessed the waters which rushed through the gorges. The park is really something of a museum of rural industrial buildings. Look out for the old weaving shed, which now houses a fascinating collection of tools. It's also worth dropping into the visitor centre, which provides information about the area's fauna and flora together with a good historical insight into the ways the water of the Roe Valley was once made to work.

Park
Open: all the time
Admission free

Visitor Centre
Open: Mon–Fri, 09.00–17.30; Sat, 12.00–17.00; Sun, 12.00–17.30
Admission free

BENONE STRAND/MAGILLIGAN STRAND

The strand ends at the tip of Magilligan Point, which reaches out into Lough Foyle. It is approached through flat lands which are bordered by brooding mountains. The fields are relatively large and fertile. The few trees to be seen clearly reveal by the way they lean that the region is regularly swept by powerful winds. The strand itself is dramatic for its sheer size. Miles of golden sand, strewn with large shells, are beaten by enormous waves. Powerful though the breakers are, when an off-shore wind is blowing they are forced back onto themselves making the spray fly high to form long foaming lines the length of the strand. In contrast, on a calm day the strand is a delightful family beach.

GORTMORE VIEWING POINT
Bishop's Road

On a fine day there are usually a few cars parked beside the handy signpost which points the way to the cliff edge; if no one seems to be around it's all too easy to wonder if they've been blown right off! This is both a very beautiful spot and an extremely windy one. However, it's well worth braving the elements for the panoramic view. Far below is Benone Strand (see above), sweeping for seven golden miles up to Magilligan Point, which is itself marked by a Martello tower. The Foyle estuary is clearly defined and on its far shore you can see the fishing port of Greencastle in County Donegal. Looking to the east you can see as far as Fair Head.

Bishop's Road, which passes across the Binevenagh Mountain, has an interesting history. It was built by the Earl Bishop of Derry as a route from Limavady to his palace at Downhill.

MUSSENDEN TEMPLE
Downhill (on cliff edge). Tel: (0265) 848281

Mussenden Temple is perhaps the most photographed monument in Northern Ireland; its image appears on many promotional leaflets and brochures. The precarious cliff edge on which it stands is reached via an attractive wild garden filled with spring flowers and rho-dodendrons, and a couple of muddy fields grazed by sheep. *En route* you will pass the burnt-out shell of Downhill Palace, which was destroyed by a fire in 1851. Directly opposite the palace's entrance is the temple, with a ha-ha between the two which was constructed to keep the sheep out.

The temple, now restored and maintained by the National Trust, is a domed rotunda whose design is based on the Temple of Vesta at Tivoli. It was constructed in 1785 by the Earl Bishop of Derry in honour of his cousin, Mrs Frideswide Mussenden, and used by him during the summer months as a library. However, if the inscription on the frieze round the dome can be believed his concentration strayed from his books for it reads, 'It is agreeable to watch, from land, someone else in a great struggle while winds whip up the waves out at sea.'

Temple	**Grounds**
Open: daily Apr–Sept, 12.00–1800	**Open:** all the time
Admission free	**Admission free** (National Trust)

HEZLETT HOUSE
Liffock, Castlerock (on A2). Tel: (0265) 848567

Hezlett House is the pretty thatched sort of dwelling that many visitors pass with a sigh wishing they could peep in through the windows, so it comes as a delightful surprise to find out that it is owned by the National Trust and is open to the public.

The house is thought to have been built in 1691 as a parsonage for the rector of Duboe. It was eventually taken over by one Isaac Hezlett, a Presbyterian farmer, whose family continued to live here for more than 200 years. Over the centuries Hezlett House has undergone a number of changes but its original construction has stood the test of time. It's made from cruck trusses, a means of building with timber frames which is not very common in the north of Ireland. A route through the house has been devised to allow visitors to walk in the roof space to see how these trusses work. There's also a useful display in one of the downstairs rooms which outlines other interesting aspects of the building. For instance, the older parts of the house are not set on foundations, instead they have been constructed on a bed of rocks. In places the restoration has been left incomplete to reveal points of interest like the hair and cow manure daub.

The house has been furnished with items from a number of periods to give a general idea of life in this type of dwelling, while outside there's a small rural garden.

Open: Wed–Mon, July and Aug, and weekends, Easter–Sept, 12.00–1.00

Admission charge (National Trust)

COUNTY ANTRIM

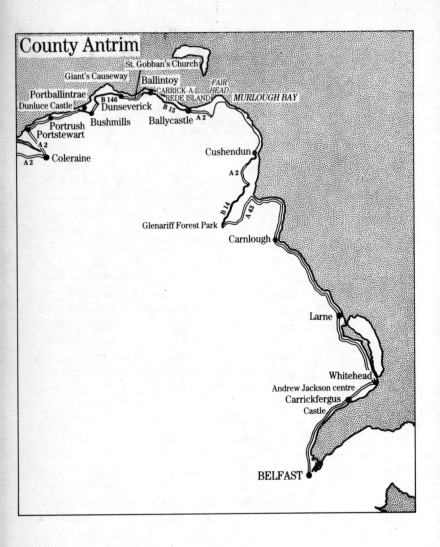

County Antrim

St. Gobban's Church
Giant's Causeway
Ballintoy
Portballintrae
Dunluce Castle
B 146
Dunseverick
CARRICK-A-
REDE ISLAND
FAIR HEAD
MURLOUGH BAY
B 15
Portrush
Bushmills
Ballycastle
A 2
Portstewart
A 2
Coleraine
A 2
Cushendun
A 2
B 14
A 43
Glenariff Forest Park
Carnlough
Larne
Whitehead
Andrew Jackson centre
Carrickfergus
Castle
BELFAST

COUNTY ANTRIM

For the most part, County Antrim is one giant undulating patchwork of fertile fields which climb high up the sides of mountains and stretch to the very edges of the region's rugged cliffs. The coast road is the county's most important attraction, it follows a route which is sometimes called a corniche – a road right on the edge of the sea. The coast road starts ignominiously enough with the harsh town of Portrush, whose streets are marred by a rash of amusement arcades, and it ends in the commercial and political realities of Belfast. However, strung out between the two is some of the loveliest and most remarkable coastal scenery to be found anywhere. Top of the bill for most visitors is the astonishing geological rock formation known as the Giant's Causeway, but there are plenty of less-well-known crags and cliffs swooping down to tiny coves and hidden harbours. The area also contains picture-postcard-pretty villages, such as Cushendun, and unremarkable market towns.

If you're travelling out of season, the roads along the coast are fairly empty, and you can take things slowly, enjoying distant views of mountains which are often snow-capped. However, if you're travelling during the summer the picture is very different. This is the main holiday spot for the north of Ireland and it is well appreciated by local people who spend their holidays here. Sundays are particularly congested days, when just about everyone seems to take to the road for a drive.

Antrim has a long history of habitation. Around 7000 BC nomadic boatsmen arrived across the water from southwest Scotland – their flint axes have been found all along the coast. Early Christians and

Vikings also colonized Antrim's shores, but it is the Normans who have left the most obvious signs of their occupation in the form of dramatically sited castles which today form romantic ruins on many cliff edges. During the late sixteenth century, the region was ruled by the MacDonnells and it is from this time that so many of the area's legends seem to date. You'll hear tales of wailing banshees, giants and ghosts, and as you explore Antrim you may well come to believe in them.

WATER WORLD
The Harbour, Portrush. Tel: (0265) 822001

This is definitely one for youngsters, or for the young at heart, at any rate. If the weather is miserable, the sea cold and the sand uninviting, give Water World a go; it's certainly a good place to warm up! As its name suggests this is a very watery attraction; in one large complex there are a whole host of water-based activities. Along with the tried and tested favourites such as the whirlpool and jacuzzi, there are all sorts of fun things to keep children busy. How about the Giant Toadstool Umbrella Shower, or the Giant Frog Slide? In this children's paradise the most popular attractions are the flumes. A powerful flow of water takes intrepid travellers on a fast and slippery journey inside a colourful coiling tube. Most people (well, children at any rate) seem to want many goes so there's often a queue, but the thrill makes the waiting all worthwhile.

Water World is a reason to visit Portrush during the day (possibly the only reason as it's spoilt by ugly developments), and right next door is the Ramore Restaurant (for bookings Tel: (0265) 824313), the reason to go at night. Many people consider the Ramore to be the best restaurant in the north of Ireland. It's highly rated in most good food guides and has been featured by Keith Floyd on television. Offering exquisitely presented courses, its food is a feast for the eye as well as the stomach.

Open: seasonal, telephone for
details
Admission charge

DUNLUCE CASTLE
5 km east of Portrush

The ruins of Dunluce Castle seem to grow out of the rocky crag on which it is built. There's little difference between the rough rock and the jagged stones, both are gradually being eroded by the pounding sea. The main part of the castle is built on an isolated rock, some 300 m high, which is separated from the mainland by a precipitous chasm. It's little wonder that some rooms of the castle actually fell off into the sea. During a storm in 1639, diners in the great hall, surprised that servants didn't come with food when called, went to search for them only to find the entire kitchen wing of the castle, including the cooks and servants, had been carried away by the sea. Today, restorers are locked in a continuous contest with the elements to save the castle from total collapse.

There are two distinct parts of Dunluce to explore; the mainland court, and the castle proper. As you arrive, the mainland court is the first part you pass through. It once provided extra space because the size of the castle was restricted by the rock on which it stands. The mainland court was also useful extra protection against surprise attack. Thick walls, known as the Funnel, lead down to what was a drawbridge but which is today a simple wooden bridge to the main fortress. Looking through crumbling windows to the powerful sea on three sides it's hard not to imagine that you're standing in the next part of the castle to be claimed by the waves.

Open: Tues–Sun, Apr–Sept, 10.00–19.00; Oct–Mar, 10.00–16.00

Admission charge

THE ULSTER WAY

The Ulster Way, one of Britain's most demanding long-distance footpaths, stretches some 896 km around Northern Ireland. It is a circular route, starting from Portballintrae, which passes through all the six counties taking walkers across lowlands and hilly landscapes, over mountains and along the coastline. The walk is divided into five sections each with trails of varying lengths. The idea is that although the real challenge of the walk is to complete it in full, you can follow parts of it for however long you choose. The waymarked route is outlined in the *Guide to the Ulster Way*, available (charge) from the Sports Council for Northern Ireland, House of Sport, Upper Malone Road, Belfast BT9 5LA. Tel: (0232) 381222.

OLD BUSHMILLS DISTILLERY
2 Distillery Road, Bushmills. Tel: (02657) 31521

The Old Bushmills Distillery is still situated on the site of the original whiskey distillery which was granted the world's first licence to distill whiskey in 1606. Parts of that first building can still be seen although they have been incorporated over the centuries into other buildings on the site. Whether or not whiskey is your favourite tipple, it's well worth taking a guided tour of Bushmills Distillery; there's so much to learn and, what's more, at the end of the tour you'll be tempted with a tasting or an aromatic hot toddy.

The raw materials of whiskey are simple enough – barley, yeast and water – but it is the secret of the processing which makes the drink special. First the ground malt (the grist) is mashed with hot water and allowed to settle in the 'mash tun'. The sugar and water solution which is produced (wort) is drawn off, cooled and put into a fermenting vessel (wash back) where yeast is added. The yeast feeds on the sugar and produces alcohol (wash). Next comes the distillation, a unique process which determines the ultimate taste of the whiskey. There follows a period of maturing in oak casks which lasts for up to ten years, followed by blending and finally bottling. Without doubt the tour will leave you with a host of images – huge copper distillation pots, a sea of tens of thousands of casks, and a memory of some very distinctive smells!

Tours: Apr–Sept, Mon–Thurs, 09.00–17.00; Fri, 09.00–12.45, booking necessary; Oct–Mar, Mon–Thurs, 11.00 and 14.30 only

Admission free (under review)

GIANT'S CAUSEWAY AND CAUSEWAY CENTRE
13 km east of Portrush. Tel: (02657) 31855

The Giant's Causeway, a promontory of basalt columns which reach out into the sea, is rightly one of Ireland's most famous tourist attractions. The columns are surprisingly symmetrical and stand bundled together like so many lead pencils. There are over 40,000 of them in all, some majestic and inaccessible in the cliff side, others easily approached along the shore. As you step from one to the next it's like walking over hundreds of piles of huge 50-pence pieces. Legend has it that the causeway, which disappears into the waves, was made by a giant named Finn MacCool. So the story goes, Finn built his amazing highway as a bridge across the sea to Scotland where there lived a lady giant with whom he was in love. And perhaps there's some substance to the tale as there are some similar columns on the island of Staffa in Fingal's cave.

In fact the columns were formed millions of years ago by volcanic activity. The lava poured out from fissures and vents in the ground at a temperature of about 1,000°C. As it spread over the white chalk it cooled and solidified into hard basalt and split to form columns; in theory the columns on cooling should all be hexagonal, and although a majority are, there are nevertheless a large minority which are pentagonal. You should also be able to spot columns which have a greater number of sides – seven and eight are not uncommon.

In the Giant's Causeway Centre you can learn much more about the geology of the area and find out too about its history as an attraction. The causeway instantly became a place to visit in 1693 when its description was published by the Royal Society. Another boost to its public profile came from the work of Susanne Drury whose paintings of the causeway were turned into engravings which were sold right across Europe. When a tramway was constructed in 1887 linking the causeway with the nearby town of Bushmills, the already famous geological feature entered its true heyday and gained a popularity which it still enjoys today. Local people were quick to cash in on the visitors, offering their services as guides and producing all manner of souvenirs. Many touted for business along the public road, as was recorded in *Ireland Illustrated* by Richard Lovett: 'The next turn down the path will bring you either to a beggar, or a seller of spring water, or a vendor of minerals of the neighbourhood.' Well, all the potential commercialization of the causeway has been confined to the centre, and its popularity can easily be judged by the large size of its car park.

Causeway	**Giant's Causeway Centre**
Open: all the time	**Open:** all year from 10.00; closes
Admission free (but fee for	19.00 July and Aug, earlier rest of
car park)	year
	Admission charge

CAUSEWAY HEADLAND WALK
Giant's Causeway to Dunseverick Castle (7 km)

If you can persuade someone to drop you off at the Giant's Causeway and collect you a few hours later at Dunseverick Castle, so much the better. However, if you're fit and keen, there's an excellent circular route (14.5 km) which is guaranteed to reward your effort.

The causeway (see p. 179) itself makes a dramatic start to the walk, which starts where the water breaks over the basalt columns. The twisting route, which winds in and out of coves, is cut into the rock face roughly mid-way between the sea and the windswept cliff top. It isn't wide, maybe as narrow as 1 m in places, so although the dangerous parts are protected by wooden fencing you do need a head for heights.

There are many geological features to look out for which have been appropriately named to describe their appearance: the Harp, the Organ, the Horse Shoe, Chimney Tops, the Camel's Back. All the time the waves beat against the rocks below while gulls circle above. The walk provides the possibility of some interesting sightings for ornithologists: there are fulmars, petrels, rock doves, gannets and eider duck along with the more common guillemots, razorbills, oystercatchers, shags and cormorants.

Two-thirds of the way along the route you'll come to a steep set of steps which lead up to Hamilton's Seat, a breathtaking viewing spot – though most of your breath will have disappeared with the climb up the steps! This is a handy place to turn back as it joins with the cliff-top walk back to the Causeway Centre. If you opt to continue, the route proceeds along the edge of fields and ends in the romantic ruins of Dunseverick Castle. Only one crumbling wall, teetering on the very edge of the cliff, remains of Dunseverick. Not much to see, perhaps, but it has a great heritage because this was once the north end of what is thought to be the oldest road in Ireland. It is here that the Celts in prehistoric times crossed to and from Scotland.

ST GOBBAN'S CHURCH
Port Bradden

Said to be the smallest church in Ireland, St Gobban's is a tiny building in a private garden. Painted puce on the outside and marked by a large bell, you can't miss it in the small harbour village of Port Bradden; there are just a handful of cottages all painted ice-cream colours at the end of a zig-zag road.

Local people enjoy a beautiful secret beach, White Park Bay, which you can see from the harbour. It's not easily reached and involves quite a walk as there's no access for cars, but at the height of the summer season it's worth the effort.

Open: only occasionally
Admission free

BALLINTOY HARBOUR

Pretty Ballintoy Harbour, at the end of a corkscrew road, is a very popular spot to take a gentle stroll. Known for its clear waters and white piers it's a tranquil place which even has the convenience of a small seasonal café. However, looks can be deceptive, on a wild day breakers crash onto the menacing black rocks of the surrounding coastline and the wind has been known to sweep a car off the pier and into the harbour.

If you fancy buying some fresh fish ask local people when the fishing boats are due and you'll be able to buy direct from the fishermen.

CARRICK-A-REDE ROPE BRIDGE
8 km west of Ballycastle (A2)

How good is your nerve? And how about your head for heights? Because Carrick-a-Rede rope bridge, although a tourist 'must', is only for the brave. A narrow bridge of roped planks is slung from the mainland to an offshore rock by fishermen. With every step you take on it, the bridge bounces alarmingly and it simultaneously sways in the wind. What's more, you only have wire handrails to cling to and the whole walk is taking place some 24 m above the sea. If you're not put off by now you should be! However, there is a pleasant 1 km walk to reach the bridge so you could just enjoy the stroll and watch others make their jittery way across the constantly swinging bridge.

Bridge assembled early May,
dismantled mid-Sept
Crossing free

MURLOUGH BAY AND FAIR HEAD WALK

Murlough Bay is situated at the end of what can truly be described as an enchanting valley. A narrow road leads down through the green folds of the valley which are grazed by sheep and decorated with beautiful trees and buttercups. At the bottom there's a sweep of beach and a lovely gentle walk.

However, if you fancy something a little more invigorating, stay at the top of the valley and walk across the cliff tops to Fair Head. The going is easy enough but you'll need tough shoes to cope with heathery bog. It's a windswept, desolate route, but it nevertheless makes for a rewarding walk as there's wildlife such as buzzards and peregrine falcons to spot and dramatic cliff scenery to be enjoyed.

From the headland there's a good view of Rathlin Island just 10 km offshore, which may be reached by boat from Ballycastle. You can also see a number of Scottish islands, which seem very near, and indeed they are because the Scottish coast is just 20 km away at this point.

CUSHENDUN

The entire village of Cushendun is now protected by the National Trust. That's because it's the work of architect Clough Williams Ellis, the man who designed Portmeirion in Wales. The architectural style of Cushendun is Cornish – rows of small whitewashed cottages with slate roofs – and Ronald McNeil, Lord Cushendun, commissioned it in honour of his Cornish wife, Maud.

Once you've wandered the main street and square there's little to do, apart, that is, from having a drink in the local pub. Cushendun boasts what is said to be the smallest pub in Ireland, McBrides. Though its recent extension makes the claim a little bit of a cheat, it's still a tight squeeze!

GLENARIFF FOREST PARK AND NATURE RESERVE

Although you have to leave the coast road to reach the glens of Antrim, it's an excursion well worth making. Best known of the glens is Glenariff, which during the summer is decked with wild flowers. To visit it take a circular route; leave the coast road at Cushendall, go up Glenballyemon to Glenariff Forest Park on the B14 and return via Glenariff on the A43.

You could easily spend two or three hours exploring the glen. The most picturesque part is the valley walk, which is canopied by lovely trees and runs alongside the river. The walk includes a number of tumbling waterfalls, which on hot days make delightful picnic spots. The forest itself hasn't been particularly cultivated, so it offers an opportunity to walk through easily accessible wild woodland along well-signed paths. If you'd like to know more about what's around you make for the visitor centre, it's packed with information and there's a handy café.

Open: daily, 10.00–dusk　　　　**Admission charge**
More information on Glens of Antrim available from: Forest Service, Dundonald House, Upper Newtownards Road, Belfast. Tel: (0323) 650111

ANDREW JACKSON CENTRE
Boneybefore. Tel: (09603) 51604

The centre is a reconstruction of a late eighteenth-century thatched cottage similar to the type the parents of Andrew Jackson, seventh President of the United States, would have lived in before they emigrated from Ireland in 1765 to start a new life in America. Standing near the site of that original house, it's an ideal home for the Andrew Jackson memorabilia and small museum devoted to his life which it contains.

Open: Easter–Sept, daily,
10.00–13.00 and 14.00–18.00;
Oct–Mar, daily 10.00–13.00 and
14.00–16.00

Admission charge

BELFAST
Tourist Information Centre, 50 High Street. Tel: (0232) 246609

Belfast is the capital city of Northern Ireland and the second largest city in the whole of Ireland. Its image is far from favourable; its recent history one of violence and division. But major redevelopment plans are underway. Buildings are being cleaned up and refurbished, new shops and offices built and more amenities provided for leisure. Take a walk through the compact city centre and you'll probably be surprised at the bright and busy atmosphere around you. Venture out further to some of the attractions (see below) on the outskirts and you'll find a wealth of historic interest and unexpected beauty. The city is surrounded by hills and hugs the shore of the Belfast Lough, and green fields can be seen from most parts of it.

Belfast is now an important industrial and commercial city, its influence spreading all over the province, but until the beginning of the nineteenth century it was just a small town of some 20,000 people with a market, harbour and scattering of housing estates. The Industrial Revolution changed the face of Belfast. Mills and factories were built and industries associated with linen, engineering and shipbuilding flourished. Harland and Wolff became the greatest shipbuilding firm in the world, producing huge ships such as the *Titanic*. The two enormous cranes, known affectionately as Goliath and Samson, still loom large over the shipyard.

Belfast grew rapidly in both prosperity and size, but expansion was in a haphazard way, the area beyond the city boundary becoming an overpopulated urban sprawl. Each district developed a strong community feel with its own traditions and character distinct from the others. In the later nineteenth century parts of the city became further segregated by religious differences. The tension continues in certain parts and can understandably put visitors off, but exercise a certain degree of caution and there is much to recommend the Port of Belfast on the River Lagan. Below are sights of special interest but you may prefer to be taken around on a bus tour. These three-and-a-half-hour tours leave from Castle Place each afternoon in the summer months, taking you via Belfast Docks and Stormont. For details contact Citybus. Tel: (0232) 246485.

Botanic Gardens. Tel: (0232) 324902. The Botanic Gardens themselves stand next to Queen's University, and boast a recently restored and restocked palm house, reputed to be one of the earliest such curvilinear glass and cast-iron structures still standing. Opposite there's a tropical ravine with views over exotic plants flourishing in their warm and balmy surroundings.

Open: all year, dawn to dusk.   **Admission free**
Tropical ravine and palm house,
Mon–Fri, 10.00–17.00; Sat and
Sun, 14.00–17.00 (closes 16.00,
Oct–Mar)

Cave Hill and Belfast Castle To the north of Stormont, Cave Hill is the home of the Belfast Zoo, and noted for its outline, known by locals as Napoleon's Nose. If time permits, the hill is worth climbing for the good views over the Lough. It was here on the summit at MacArt's Fort that Wolfe Tone, Henry Joy McCracken and other United Irishmen gathered together in 1798 to take an oath of allegiance to a United Ireland. Nearby are five man-made caves, dating back to Neolithic times. At the foot of the hill stands the baronial Belfast

Castle, surrounded by a wooded estate. Although you can walk through the grounds, the castle is only open for functions.

Open: all the time
Admission free

City Hall, Donegall Square. Tel: (0232) 320202. This impressive white Portland stone building is one of the city's major landmarks and quite splendid. Its graceful copper dome towers some 53 m high offering splendid views and making it hard to miss. Built in 1896–1906 it is in Renaissance style, each of its corners having a tower. The old White Linen Hall originally stood on the site but when Belfast was declared a city in 1888, the city fathers demanded it be replaced with a new city hall. Its grandeur is a reflection of the wealth and optimistic air of Belfast at the time, a special feature is the large mural depicting Belfast's industrial history. Entry into the sumptuous interiors of the council chamber, oak-panelled banqueting hall and other stately halls smothered in multi-coloured Italian marble, is by guided tour only.

Open: all year, tour Wed, 10.30, or
by arrangement. Must be booked in
advance

Crown Liquor Saloon, Great Victoria Street. Across the road from the lavishly decorated Grand Opera House is this unusual pub now in the hands of the National Trust. Described by John Betjeman as a 'many coloured cavern', the richness of the ornamentation in the gas-lit interior is quite amazing. You'll find yourself so fascinated with the detailing of the decoration a drink will last a long time. Formerly a railway hotel, it was built in around 1885 during Belfast's prosperous years, and has a strong Italian influence.

Stormont Buildings, Dundonald. Tel: (0232) 63210. Stormont stands proudly at the end of a long processional avenue in Stormont Park, just 8 km from the city centre. Built in 1928–32 it once housed the parliament and certain government ministries of Northern Ireland. A statue of Lord Carson of Duncairn, leader of the movement that kept Northern Ireland in the United Kingdom, stands in front of the building while in the entrance hall there's a statue of Lord Craigavon, the first prime minister.

Open: interior by special request
only
Admission free

Transport Museum, Witham Street. Tel: (0232) 451519. Although very compact, this museum, an offshoot of the Ulster Folk and Transport Museum (see p. 194), boasts a fine collection of well-restored vehicles tracing the history of Irish transport over 200 years. There are steam locomotives, street trams and road vehicles with exhibits ranging from the biggest locomotive ever built in Ireland, Old Meave, which weighs a massive 135 tons, to the smallest car, made for Davy Jones, the smallest man in the world.

Open: all year, Mon–Sat,
10.00–17.00
Admission charge

Ulster Museum and Art Gallery, Botanic Gardens. Tel: (0232) 668251. This vast museum's setting in the Botanic Gardens is delightful and the exhibits most impressive. There are fine collections of anti-quities illustrating the history of Northern Ireland but you'll also find sections devoted to botany, zoology, geology, technology and much more. It seems, happily, to go on for ever. Among the more recent additions are the gold, jewellery and other treasures salvaged from the *Girona*, the Spanish galleon which sank off Lacada Point, County Antrim, in 1588. The museum holds lectures, film shows and changing exhibitions. Attached is an art gallery with works by leading Belfast-born artists such as Sir John Lavery, Paul Henry and William Conor.

Open: all year, Mon–Fri,   **Admission free**
10.00–17.00; Sat 13.00–17.00; Sun
14.00–17.00

THE RAILWAY PRESERVATION
SOCIETY OF IRELAND
Whitehead Excursion Station, Castleview Road, Whitehead.
Tel: (09603) 78567

There's something very special about seeing and hearing a powerful steam-engine in action. Here at Whitehead there's the chance to get a close-up view of a steam locomotive and also to experience the elegance of rail travel in the years between 1920 and 1950 when trains were steam-hauled and coaches had polished wood interiors. The Railway Preservation Society of Ireland (RPSI) has collected and restored nine steam locomotives, two diesels, over thirty coaches and a collection of goods vehicles, most of which are stored and worked on at Whitehead. Steam events are held on Sundays during July and for children Easter Bunny Train and Santa Train rides are always popular and very reasonably priced. The RPSI also organize summer excursion train rides from other points in Northern Ireland. Ask for details.

Open: rides on selected days, telephone or write (enclose sae) for details. Viewing by arrangement on other days.

Admission charge

CARRICKFERGUS CASTLE
Carrickfergus. Tel: (09603) 51273

For many people the highlight of a visit to this magnificent castle, standing on a rocky peninsula beside the harbour, is the dark and eerie dungeon, guaranteed to fire the imagination. Among the many notable prisoners was Con O'Neill of Castlereagh who, so the story goes, escaped using a rope hidden in a cheese smuggled in by his wife. Carrickfergus Castle was built around 1180 by John de Courcy, the first of the Anglo-Norman invaders of Ulster, to guard the approach to Belfast Lough.

A booklet, obtainable at the reception, describes the turbulent history of the castle, which was in military occupation for 750 years, and outlines the main points of interest today: the 11 m deep well; the portcullis with its ancient machinery; the splendid Great Hall; and the armour, weapons, uniforms and other exhibits in the military museums. Look out, too, for the plaque at the end of the quay which marks the spot where William of Orange landed in 1690 on his way to the Battle of the Boyne. Medieval banquets are held in the castle, and on 1 August the town's colourful Lughnasa Fair, a medieval fair, is held around the battlements.

While in Carrickfergus, it's also worth visiting St Nicholas's Church, built around the same time as the castle, with the monument to Sir Arthur Chichester, Governor of Carrickfergus, who died in 1625.

Castle
Open: Apr–Sept, Mon–Sat, 10.00–18.00; Sun, 14.00–18.00; Oct–Mar, Mon–Sat, 10.00–16.00; Sun, 14.00–16.00. Last admission half an hour before closing. Other times by arrangement.

Admission charge

COUNTY DOWN

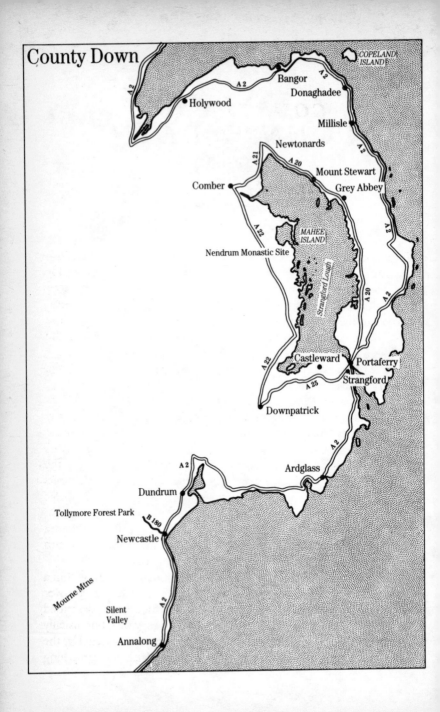

COUNTY DOWN

Throughout history the County of Down, bordered by sea and close to both Scotland and England, has been a natural landing point for Ireland's many invaders, most notably the plundering Vikings who began their raids along the east coast from Down in the ninth century. Earlier, in the fifth century, the county received another visitor, the missionary bishop Patrick who travelled Ireland converting the people to Christianity. Downpatrick, the burial place of St Patrick, is just one of the many places in Down boasting strong links with the country's patron saint.

North Down is fertile country with gently sloping hills which C. S. Lewis, a native of Down, sums up so graphically in his autobiography as a layer of earth-covered potatoes. It also boasts one of the sunniest and driest climates in the north. On the east shore is the Ards Peninsula pointing down like a finger between the sea and the beautiful nearly land-locked Strangford Lough. Named Ards after its rocky shoreline (ard means rock), it is skirted by a particularly scenic coastal road. The winding route takes you past charming fishing villages such as Portavogie, famed for its prawns, small towns dotted with white thatched cottages, sandy beaches, conservation areas and enough antiquities from past ages to fill a history book.

Further south are the mighty Mourne Mountains which, within a circuit of only 40 km have some 48 peaks, 15 of which rise to over 600 m above sea level. These heather-covered mountains, described by C. S. Lewis as sometimes blue, sometimes violet but usually transparent, are strangely calm and peaceful. They are bisected by the lovely Carlingford Lough, a long arm of the Irish Sea stretching inland to the large industrial centre and port of Newry. Historically Newry is important because of its position at what is known as the 'Gap of the North', the main route between the north and the south of Ireland. To the west of Newry is Slieve Gullion, 'Ireland's mountain of mystery', which is at the centre of many ancient tales.

ULSTER FOLK AND TRANSPORT MUSEUM
Cultra, Nr Holywood. Tel (0232) 428428

This is no ordinary museum, it's a huge open-air folk park which takes you on a journey back in time to show the traditional way of life in Ulster over the past couple of centuries. Visitors are directed straight to Cultra Manor, a visitor centre with exhibitions showing domestic life and farming practices over the years. Then with map in hand you're free to wander, but do save plenty of time because you'll want to see it all.

The park, which covers some 136 acres, is set in beautiful surroundings dotted with important examples of vernacular buildings, carefully moved stone by stone from different parts of Ulster and re-erected here at Cultra. The crops in the fields are still harvested in the traditional way. You can look around old farmhouses, cottages, watermills, a small village with a church, shops, a school and a terrace of industrial workers' houses. Other buildings on view range from a tiny one-roomed dwelling to a large early eighteenth-century rectory. Each building has been painstakingly refurnished so you get the feeling that the owners have just popped out and will be back shortly. Some buildings have an attendant on duty to answer any questions.

The Transport Galleries tell the story of transport right up to the present day with exhibits as diverse as a donkey creel, three-masted schooner and a modern prototype of a military vertical-take-off-and-landing aircraft. A miniature steam-engine runs from outside the galleries at weekends.

Open: Apr–Sept, Mon–Sat,
11.00–18.00; Sun, 14.00–18.00;
(May and June, Wed, open until
21.00); Oct–Apr, Mon–Sat,
11.00–17.00; Sun, 14.00–17.00

Admission charge

DONAGHADEE

Standing beside Donaghadee Harbour you are just 34 km from Scotland. This is the nearest Irish port to Great Britain and naturally has many associations with its Scottish counterpart, Portpatrick. The route between the two ports not only brought mail packets but also several famous visitors, including James Boswell and also John Keats who arrived in 1818 intending to walk to the Giant's Causeway (see p. 179) but he stopped at Belfast (see p. 184). Donaghadee is no longer a major port but it is a delightful place to visit and a lovely spot for a picnic or walk. Look out for local boatmen gathering dulse at low tide. This edible seaweed, which is dried and eaten raw or cooked in bacon fat, is a traditional delicacy in Ireland. Other attractions include the lighthouse and the rath, known as the Moat, with a nineteenth-century castellated powder house on top. This was used to store explosives when the harbour was being built.

To the northwest of the harbour are the Copeland Islands, which can be reached by a regular boat service. The largest, Big Isle, was inhabited until the 1940s and is still used as a weekend retreat by some. It is around 1.5 km from Donaghadee, the stretch of water making a perfect distance for the swimming races that are held from time to time. Further on is Cross, or Lighthouse Island (it keeps its name although there's no longer a lighthouse here), now a bird observatory. The outermost island is Mew with the present-day lighthouse.

BALLYCOPELAND WINDMILL
1.5 km west of Millisle. Tel: (0232) 230560

There were once over a hundred windmills in East Down, tradition-ally a good grain-growing area. Windmill stumps are a familiar sight dotted around the county but the cornmill at Ballycopeland is now the only working windmill left in the whole of Ireland. A photograph inside shows just how derelict it was in 1935 before the restoration work began and its excellent condition today is a tribute to the patience and skill of dedicated craftsmen.

The white-painted mill, which stands on a small hill a mile inland from the seaside resort of Millisle, makes a splendid landmark for miles around. It is a tower-type mill with a movable cap turned by an automatic fantail so the sails always face the wind. It was built in the 1780s or 1790s of local stone and used for milling oats and wheat and making animal feed right up until just after the Second World War. The main beam is still the original one, made from the mast of a ship found in Millisle. A detailed plan shows what is on view on each floor and explains the different terms, milling techniques and workings of the intricate wooden machinery. Several tools found nearby are also on display, including an old stone-chipper used for roughing up the grinding stones when they became too smooth.

Open: Apr–Sept, Tues–Sat, 10.00–19.00; Sun, 14.00–19.00; Oct–Mar, Sat, 10.00–16.00; Sun, 14.00–16.00. Or by arrangement. Closed 13.00–13.30

Admission charge

STRANGFORD LOUGH

The abundance of wildlife of all shapes and forms in and around this great lough, an inlet of the Irish Sea, is a quite unexpected delight. Noted for its fish, particularly the great skate, it is also one of the most important bird sanctuaries in Britain, providing a temporary home for birds travelling between the tropics and the Arctic. The species change with the seasons so there's always something new to see. More permanent residents are the terns, gulls and oystercatchers and other waders who breed on the many islands in the lough. The lough is especially busy in the winter months when great flocks of brent geese and other species arrive. It is also a centre of marine life with over 2,000 species recorded, including starfish, sponges, scale worms and sea squirts. From the Cloghy Rocks you can watch seals (as many as 600 are here during the summer) basking in the warmth on the rocks while the roadside and the numerous drumlins, or Ice Age hillocks, near the shore are rich with wild flowers, many, such as the green-winged orchid, rare and beautiful.

So why is this shallow stretch of water, 32 km long and up to 5 km wide, such a haven for wildlife? A clue lies in its name. It was called Strangford by the Vikings, the word meaning 'violent fjord', because of the strength with which the water gushes in through its narrow entrance. This fierce rush of water brings with it a continuous source of nutrients to feed its marine life. The green and fertile shores surrounded by wooded estates and the tiny isolated islands within the lough all play their part in providing suitable and relatively undisturbed natural habitats.

To find out more about the lough, one of the first places to visit should be the **Northern Ireland Aquarium** at Portaferry. Well-lit spacious tanks give a real insight into life under the water of the lough while an imaginative exhibition is full of all those facts and figures that children seem to love – Britain's heaviest lobster (over 18 kg) was caught in the lough, for example, and 350 million tonnes of sea-water flow into Strangford Lough with each high tide.

For a close-up view of the wildfowl of the area, make for the **Castle Espie Conservation Centre** and Gallery, a sanctuary and breeding ground for ducks, geese and swans from all over the world. Visitors to the Observation Room are provided with binoculars and reference books. If you'd rather venture further out, there's a hide in the pine wood just beyond the gallery.

The best overall view of the lough is from the top of **Scrabo Tower** (there are 122 steps to climb!), 3 km west of Newcastle. The tower, built in 1857 as a memorial to the Third Marquis of Londonderry, is now a countryside centre.

All around the lough there are places of historic interest: Grey Abbey (see p. 198), Mount Stewart (see p. 199), Nendrum Monastic Site (see p. 200) and Castle Ward (see p. 203). Once known as the Quiet Lough for reasons obvious to the visitor, it is both relaxing and exciting to visit, especially for newcomers who can never be quite sure what they'll see or stumble across next.

Northern Ireland Aquarium,
Portaferry. Tel: (02477) 28062
Open: Apr–July, Tues–Sat,
10.00–20.00; Sun, 13.00–20.00;
Sept–Mar, Tues–Sat, 10.30–17.00;
Sun, 13.00–17.00
Admission charge

**Castle Espie Conservation Centre
and Gallery,** 78 Ballydrain Road,
Comber. Tel: (0247) 872517
Open: all year, Wed–Sat and Bank
Hols, 10.30–17.00
Admission charge

Scrabo Tower, near Newcastle
Open: Easter–Sept, Wed–Mon,
12.00–17.30. Or by arrangement
Admission free

PORTAFERRY–STRANGFORD FERRY
Tel: (039 686) 637

The two pretty villages of Strangford and Portaferry are at the mouth of the lough, separated by a narrow strait where water gushes through at a tremendous pace. The crossing is short, only five minutes in all, but the scenery is stunning. The continuous click of cameras by those on board say it all. Essentially a functional car and passenger ferry service, it's worth making the trip forward and back purely for pleasure. There are splendid views of the wooded shores of the lough and of the waterfront of Portaferry with its cottages, pubs and shops.

Open: all year, daily at half-hour
intervals
Admission charge

GREY ABBEY
East of Greyabbey village

A quiet and solemn air still fills this Cistercian monastery. It is so peaceful, amid grounds bursting with trees and flowers, that it's lovely just to wander around these extensive ruins and conjure up pictures of the past life here. The abbey was founded in 1193 by Affreca (an effigy tomb in the north wall of the choir is thought to be hers) who was daughter of the king of the Isle of Man and wife of John de Courcy, Norman conqueror of Ulster.

Grey Abbey was the daughter house of Holm Cultram in Cumbria. At the time of its foundation, the Normans were wary of the Irish church and its connections with local clan chiefs, so they brought monks over from England to found the new abbeys. The link between Grey Abbey and Holm Cultram remained strong for several hundred years; monks from Grey Abbey would take boats across to Cumbria stocked with corn, wheat, flour and other provisions and return home with stone and iron ore. The abbey was burned out in 1572 but it was reroofed as a parish church by the Montgomery family, from nearby Rosemount House, and used for worship right up until the late eighteenth century. Inside, there are some notable memorials – look at the inscriptions, they make interesting reading.

Open: Apr–Sept, Tues–Sat, 10.00–19.00; Sun 14.00–19.00; Oct–Mar, Sat, 10.00–16.00; Sun, 14.00–16.00. Or by arrangement. Closed 13.00–13.30

Admission charge

MOUNT STEWART HOUSE AND GARDENS
8 km southeast of Newtownards on A20. Tel: (024 774) 387

The gardens are the main attraction at Mount Stewart. Their beauty, in fact, rather overshadows the attraction of the house, birthplace of Lord Castlereagh (1769–1822), British foreign secretary during the Napoleonic Wars. Although the interior is finely decorated and furnished and of historic interest, it's the unexpected loveliness of the gardens, famed for rhododendrons and rare trees and flowers, which people remember. It's difficult to take it all in at first. It's exhausting just thinking about all the painstaking work and horticultural skills invested in creating such an abundance of imaginative themes and collections; indeed, there's just about every style of gardening in evidence at Mount Stewart. To enjoy the gardens just let the paths lead you to surprise after surprise, to magnificent vistas and unusual displays of colour.

The gardens were laid out in the early 1920s by Lady Londonderry to give her children pleasure. Today, her eccentric touches delight visiting adults as much as children. The statues, all made by local craftspeople, are particularly popular. There's a menagerie of stone figures, including dinosaurs, dodos, lions, crocodiles, monkeys and a cat playing a fiddle. There's also a white stag standing in a glade, created to be seen to full effect by the light of the moon. And anyone who has tried just to clip a hedge will be fascinated by the topiary art, with masterpieces ranging from an Irish harp to a full-scale hunt.

Different sections of the gardens are devoted to certain themes and colours. Bold and vivid, the 'Red Hand' of Ulster, for example, is created from careful planting of red-leaved plants. Among the other themes are a sunken garden, Spanish garden and Italian garden. A special feature is the eighteenth-century folly known as the Temple of the Winds. A copy of a temple in Athens, this octagonal building was originally used as a banqueting hall. From inside, the views over the lough are breathtaking.

Open: Apr, weekends, 14.00–18.00; May, Wed–Sun, 14.00–18.00; June–Aug, daily (except Mon), 12.00–18.00; Sept, daily (except Mon) until mid-Sept, and weekends, 14.00–18.00; Oct, weekends, 14.00–18.00. Gardens and temple also open at other times.

Admission charge (National Trust)

NENDRUM MONASTIC SITE
Mahee Island, Comber

Isolated is perhaps the best word to describe the location of this early monastic site, standing on a grassy hill on Mahee Island just south of Comber on the west shore of the lough. As the road twists and winds along the narrow causeway it's rather like a mystery tour – the views across the lough are splendid, certainly, but just what will you find at the end of it all? It was the lonely setting that so attracted the early monks, searching for a life of solitude, and it's the same sense of isolation that makes Nendrum such a romantic place to visit today.

The original founder is believed to be the fifth-century St Mochaoi (Mahee), a convert of St Patrick. Legend has it that he worked so hard in building the church that when he heard the song of a heavenly bird in the forest, he fell asleep for 150 years. Records show that by the seventh century Nendrum was an active monastic house. It became a parish church in 1300 but was moved to the mainland in the fifteenth century. The site was only rediscovered in 1844 and extensive excavations, begun in 1922, are still unearthing new finds. Among the more important treasures is the monastic bell, which is now in the Ulster Museum in Belfast (see p. 187).

The site is beautiful and the remains made fascinating by the lively and well-researched information plaques – visitors are told of dramatic events such as the day in 976 AD when the Abbot of Nendrum was burned alive in his own house in a Viking raid. Illustrations on display give a vivid idea of how the buildings would have been laid out at the time. There would have been three concentric enclosures defined by drystone walls high enough to provide defence. The outer cashel (stone fort) would probably have enclosed some 6 acres and would have crops, pastureland, dwellings and a guest house. The middle cashel on the west side enclosed around 1½ acres. Excavations have uncovered monks' huts and workshops including a smithy and pottery here. The inner cashel contained the most important buildings: the church, graveyard and monastic belfry (round tower), remains of which can be seen. Look out too for the early sundial, once used for timing services.

Ruins
Open: all the time
Admission free

Interpretative Centre
Open: Apr–Sept, daily,
10.00–19.00
Admission free

DOWNPATRICK

Down Cathedral, ransacked, burnt and rebuilt through the ages, still stands as the centrepiece of the hilly town of Downpatrick. Here, in the graveyard, St Patrick is reputed to be buried, his bones lying with those of two other great saints, Columba and Brigid. A rather unimpressive slab of granite with the simple inscription 'PATRIC' marks the site. It's not immediately obvious so you may need to ask its location. On St Patrick's Day (17 March) pilgrims make their way to the cathedral and throw daffodils onto the grave. St Patrick, Ireland's patron saint, was born in South Wales in around 389 AD. It's said that he was brought over to Ireland as a young boy, having been captured as a slave in a pirate raid, but later escaped. He returned to Ireland in 432 AD as a bishop, landing at Slaney River, and preached his first sermon on Irish soil at Saul, just 3 km north of Downpatrick. An imposing 11 m high granite statue of St Patrick on Slieve Patrick looks down over the valley and nearby are the Holy Wells at Struell, said to have miraculous healing powers.

Down Museum and Heritage Centre, The Mall. Tel: (039 66) 15218. In a town so strongly linked to St Patrick, it comes as no surprise to find a Heritage Centre devoted to telling the story of Ireland's patron saint. The small museum aims to tell the truth behind the many romantic myths. A creditable objective certainly, but also difficult to achieve as there are only two documents attributable to St Patrick to work on. However, large-scale illustrations help paint a picture of life in this part of Ireland during the time of St Patrick. The Heritage Centre is housed within the gatehouses of the high wall that once surrounded the old Down County Gaol. Built in 1789–96, the gaol complex has been recently restored and is the most complete example of its type still in existence. The red brickwork over the front gateway shows the entrance to what was once the gaol gallows. From here, the gaol's most famous prisoner, the United Irishman Thomas Russell, was hanged in 1803. The building is also the home of the Down Museum with exhibits tracing the history of County Down from the Stone Age.

Down Museum and St Patrick Heritage Centre, The Mall. **Open:** July–Aug, Tues–Fri, 11.00–17.00; Sat, 14.00–17.00; Sun, 14.00–18.00

Admission free

CASTLE WARD
2.5 km west of Strangford. Tel: (039 686) 204

No one seems entirely sure who designed Castle Ward, although many say that, like the stone of the house, the architect came from Bath or Bristol. One thing is for certain, though; he was very adaptable. Commissioned in the 1760s by Bernard Ward, later the first Lord Bangor, and his wife, 'the whimsical Lady Anne', he had to allow for their widely differing tastes and opinions. Much to the amusement of visiting couples, Castle Ward is a perfect compromise between the Palladian style preferred by Ward and the fashionable Gothic his wife favoured. Even the interior keeps cleverly in style. You'll spot the warring couple's personal rooms immediately – elaborate and extravagant for the lady, classical and restrained for the lord.

Castle Ward is set in such an idyllic spot overlooking Strangford Lough that many people come just to enjoy the grounds. It's particularly beautiful in the spring when the fields are a carpet of yellow daffodils and bright bluebells, but thanks to the mild climate, rare and exotic plants, trees and shrubs flourish and there's something to see whatever the season. The gardens are full of interest – a wildfowl lake, a temple folly, a small theatre in a converted barn, a Victorian laundry room with a stone mangle, old irons and carefully laundered clothes, and a farmyard with buildings including a corn mill and saw mill, both restored, and a seventeenth-century tower house.

House
Open: Apr weekends, 14.00–18.00; May, Wed–Sun and Bank Hols, 14.00–18.00; June–Aug, daily (except Tues), 12.00–18.00; Sept–Oct, weekends, 14.00–18.00
Admission charge (National Trust)

Grounds
Open: all year, daily, dawn to one hour before dusk
Admission free

DUNDRUM CASTLE
Dundrum. Tel: (0232) 230560

Standing high on a wooded hill to the northwest of Dundrum village is a fine Norman castle, one of the coastal defences that controlled the shoreline from Greencastle, on Carlingford Lough, to Carrickfergus (see p. 188). Despite being the focus of many violent attacks in the past, the castle still boasts a huge and remarkably well-preserved keep and has many features of interest including a latrine in the outer wall and an impressive Elizabethan gateway. However, for many visitors the greatest attraction is its picturesque setting. The views from the car park across Dundrum Bay are quite breathtaking and if you've time to explore the footpaths down by the bay you'll be well-rewarded. From here you can spot the seals and birds that have settled among the sand dunes and heathland in the Murlough National Nature Reserve, Ireland's first such reserve.

Castle
Open: Apr–Sept, Mon–Sat, 10.00–19.00; Sun, 14.00–16.00; Oct–Mar, Tues–Sat, 10.00–16.00; Sun, 14.00–16.00 (closed 13.00–13.30)
Admission charge

Nature Reserve: Public walkways open all the time. Guided walks and Information Centre, daily, May–Sept
Admission free

TOLLYMORE FOREST PARK
176 Tullybrannigan Road, Newcastle. Tel: (039 67) 22428

Set at the foot of the Mourne Mountains, Tollymore was the first forest park in Northern Ireland, opened in 1955. Motorists enter by the Barbican Gate (off the Newcastle to Bryansford Road) and then after driving along the picturesque avenue of Himalayan cedars, you are asked to leave your car in the car park and discover the rest of the 2,000 acre park on foot. There are many different places to explore, spectacular viewpoints and an abundance of wildlife to enjoy, indeed it's difficult to know where to head first. However, with a café, picnic spots and even camping and caravan sites (book in high season on the above telephone number), you can extend your visit for as long as you wish.

To help visitors see the main points of interest there are a series of forest trails signposted from the car park. The shortest is just under a mile, taking you through the Azalea Walk along a stretch of the Shimna River to the Hermitage and back alongside the Forest Garden. The longest, the Long Haul Trail, is for the more energetic walker. Fourteen km long, it takes you well away from the popular routes and gives you the opportunity to enjoy the panoramic views from the highest point in the park. On a clear day you can see as far as the Isle of Man.

Of special note is the Arboretum, to the west of the car park, where specimen tree planting began over 200 years ago. All the trees are carefully labelled, some are original, others have been added to ensure a good representation of tree species and shrubs. Look out for the wild strawberry tree (the fruit is not at all tasty!), the huge Monterey pine and the sequoia tree, which is over 30 m tall. An eighteenth-century barn has been restored to provide space for exhibitions. The park also offers pony trekking and game fishing (permit required).

Open: all the time
Admission free

SILENT VALLEY RESERVOIR
Mourne Mountains. Tel: (039 67) 62121

The drive from Newcastle to Warrenpoint is dominated by the Mourne Mountains, which true to the words of the celebrated song by Percy French really do 'sweep down to the sea'. Indeed, the highest of the peaks, Slieve Donard (852 m), is only 2.5 km from the coast. There's only one road across the mountains, Spelga Dam, and although there are access points for walkers and climbers in the foothills, the Silent Valley Reservoir is the only place in the high peaks that vehicles can reach. There are several roads there off the main A2 but signposting is not always all it should be, and it's easy to miss your turn, so do study a map first. A good road to take is just ½ km north of the harbour and seaside town of Annalong.

The driveway takes you up through countryside dotted with

grazing sheep, whitewashed cottages and fields bounded by drystone walls and into an oasis of lush greenery and colourful plants. Leave your car in the car park and explore the impressive reservoir and its lovely surroundings on foot. An information plaque explains the work of the reservoir while in the information centre displays tell the story of the building of the dam. The reservoir, which has the capacity to hold 3,000 million gallons of water, consists of two artificial lakes and supplies 30 million gallons of water to Belfast and environs every day. The rough stone Mourne Wall surrounding Silent Valley runs up and down as many as fifteen mountains and stretches for just over 35 km.

Open: Apr–Oct, daily,   **Admission free**
10.00–17.00; Nov–Mar,
10.00–16.00

ANNALONG CORNMILL
Marine Park, Annalong. Tel: (039 67) 68736

Right up until the 1960s this early nineteenth-century cornmill was operated commercially. Today, however, it is restored and preserved as a working museum. Annalong is a water-powered mill, and the highlight of a visit is seeing its water wheel in action. The wheel is operated by water from the River Annalong; you can take a walk along its bank to the weir – part of the water power system. To see the rest of the mill you must join a guided tour. The tour is very informative. It takes about 45 minutes for the guide to explain all the milling processes and for you to see all there is to see. It includes a look at the grain drying kiln, hopper and sack hoist. You also get the chance to grind a little corn yourself, in the old-fashioned way with a handmill – it provides a clear insight into why hydraulic power was so very important.

Open: June–Aug, 14.00–18.00
Admission charge

COUNTY LOUTH

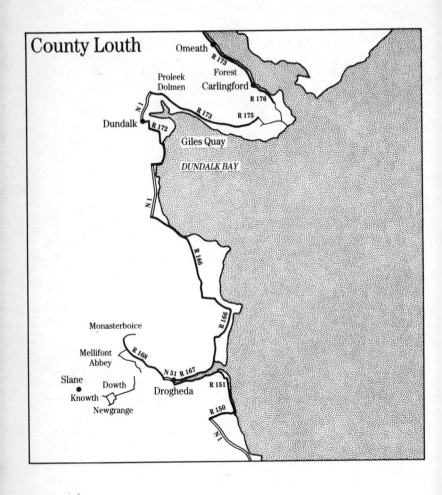

COUNTY LOUTH

Louth is the smallest county in Ireland. Its 810 square km stretch from the scenic Carlingford Lough on the Northern Ireland border to the mouth of the River Boyne. To the north is the wild and beautiful Cooley Peninsula. Known as Cuchulainn's Country, the heather-covered hills are said to be the birthplace of Ireland's most famous warrior. The rugged countryside is the setting for many of Ireland's ancient sagas of kings and heroes and their battles. The most famous of these Iron Age epics is the 'Tain Bo Cuailnge', 'The Cattle Raid of Cooley', which is set in the town of Ardee.

As the coast road leads down to Drogheda, the scenery changes completely, the hills giving way to sandy beaches, small farms and secluded fishing villages. The ancient town of Drogheda is now a major port and also a gateway to the Boyne Valley, which stretches into the neighbouring County Meath. The vista is gloriously fresh and green, and the narrow roads along the Boyne Valley lead you from one peaceful spot to another. It is hard to imagine that this was the site of one of Ireland's most momentous battles, the Battle of the Boyne. This battle in 1690 changed the course of Irish history when the Protestant William of Orange defeated the Catholic James II of England.

Louth and its neighbouring county, Meath, are rich in ancient ruins and historic spots, reflecting almost every period of the country's history from the first inhabitants of the Mesolithic era whose remains have been found near the coast at Drogheda. Although not inhabited at such an early date, the village of Mell near Drogheda can also claim the oldest object made by man yet to be found in Ireland – a flint shaped in Palaeolithic times.

COOLEY PENINSULA

The east coast of Ireland, although blessed with fertile plains, seems to have missed out on the wild and rugged beauty of so many other parts of the country. However, this mountainous peninsula of granite rock overlooking Carlingford Lough is an exception, its unspoilt beauty having more in common with the west than the east. Dundalk Bay lies to the south and to the north is Carlingford Lough with the famous Mourne Mountains reflected in the water.

The coastline around the peninsula stretches for some 50 km with plenty of places of interest, information points, picnic spots and fine views. Start the tour at the small resort of Omeath, once a Gaeltacht village, the only one in the province. An excellent place to buy fresh shellfish, it is famed for the much-visited Calvary Shrine, a series of open-air Stations of the Cross representing the Passion. Jaunting cars (pony and trap) take visitors from the beach to the shrine about 1.5 km east of the village. For wonderful views of the lough, across to the Mountains of Mourne and the coast of County Down, it's worth taking a detour along the narrow mountain road to the intriguing-sounding Long Woman's Grave.

The medieval village of Carlingford with its harbour, narrow winding streets, whitewashed cottages and traditional pubs is the next stop. Full of castellated buildings (at one time there were as many as thirty-two!), it is steeped in historic interest. The village, famed for its oysters in season, is dramatically situated at the foot of Slieve Foye, which looks far higher than its 590 m. It is also the start of the Tain Way, a 30 km walking trail which takes you high up into the Cooley Mountains. Three kilometres to the west is **Carlingford Forest Park** with picnic sites, walks and a viewing point near the top of the mountains.

The southern side of the peninsula is less scenic that the north although Giles Quay has a good beach with lovely views across to Dunany Point and Clogher Head. Further along the road to Dundalk at Ballymascanlon is the **Proleek Dolmen.** This huge burial monument dating back to around 3,000 BC is freely accessible from a path leading behind the Ballymascanlon House Hotel. Known locally as the 'Giant's Load', the mighty capstone weighs over 46 tonnes supported by two 1 m high stones. Head on to **Faughart**, an early Christian monastic site reputed to be the birthplace of St Brigid, Patroness of Ireland. On Faughart Hill is a cemetery where Edward Bruce, brother of Robert Bruce, was buried in 1318, killed in battle nearby. It is, however, the panoramic views that hold the real attraction. The whole of Leinster is spread out before you.

Carlingford Forest Park
Open: daily, dawn to dusk
Admission free

Faughart
Open: all the time
Admission free

Proleek Dolmen
Open: all the time
Admission free

DUNDALK
Tourist Information: Market Square. Tel: (042) 35484

Dundalk, the county town of Louth, is a busy manufacturing centre and seaport. It is not pretty or particularly pleasing to wander through but it is historically important, its origins dating right back to the prehistoric ring fort of Dun Dealgan (Delga's Fort) built to guard the gap in the mountains known as 'The Gap of the North'. Its development as a town dates back to the late twelfth century when a settlement grew up around the large motte and bailey built by the Anglo-Norman de Vere, the king's appointed Lord of the Liberty of Meath. The town later moved to the flat lands on the seashore. Repeatedly burned and attacked over five centuries, there's little now left to remind visitors of the town's stormy past. However, the large and well-stocked tourist information centre has plenty of literature to help visitors find their way around the region.

One of the oldest buildings in Dundalk is **Seatown Castle**, which despite the name is actually the bell tower of an early thirteenth-century Franciscan monastery. Perhaps the most spectacular building is the **Courthouse**, a stern Greek revival building of the 1820s. The **Pro-Cathedral of St Patrick** was built several years later in 1837–48 from Newry granite. The exterior is a copy of the chapel of King's College, Cambridge. The **Church of St Nicholas** is famed for its interesting sixteenth-century tombs. Agnes Galt, sister of the poet Robert Burns, is buried in the graveyard there. Dundalk also boasts a windmill, **Seatown Windmill**, which is reputed to be the largest in Ireland although it is no longer working. A major landmark in Dundalk is the **P.J. Carroll and Co.** tobacco factory on the main Dublin Road. Visitors are invited to step behind its fascinating facade and find out how tobacco is manufactured.

Seatown Castle
Open: all the time
Admission free

The Courthouse
The exterior only can be viewed

**Pro-Catholic Cathedral of
St Patrick**
Open: daily
Admission free

Seatown Windmill
The exterior only can be viewed

P. J. Carroll and Co. Tel: (042) 36501
Open: factory tours on request
Admission free

MONASTERBOICE

The isolated setting within an old graveyard makes the beauty of the ruins even more dramatic. There are no guides to rush you or set routes to follow. Explanatory boards help fill in the background information without being obtrusive, leaving you free to soak up the atmosphere of this early Christian monastic settlement at your leisure. The monastery was founded by St Buithe (Boice) in the late fifth century. Little is known about the saint, although he is said to have died in 521 AD on the day that St Columb was born.

Monasterboice was never plundered like so many Irish monasteries, but sadly, the abbey and great library of treasures were destroyed by fire. But much still remains to be seen. The glory of the ruins are the

Celtic crosses. Indeed, if they look familiar it's probably because the three magnificent ornamented crosses at Monasterboice are the subject of so many photographs. The tenth-century cross of Muireadach is particularly impressive; just look at the detailed carving, which has weathered remarkably well. The cross stands 5.4 m high and is almost completely covered with sculptured panels, richly ornamented with Celtic tracery and abstract design, depicting scenes from the Bible. Scriptural crosses such as these are known as 'books in stone'; the carvings once helped illiterate people to understand the Scriptures.

Other remains of interest are the walls and gables of two old churches and a ninth-century round tower, probably one of the tallest in Ireland in its day. The entrance, 2 m above the ground, was once reached by removable stairs, but today there are steps for visitors wishing to explore inside. There's also an ornate sundial, near the North Cross, and two early grave slabs.

Open: all the time
Admission free

MELLIFONT ABBEY
Collon. Tel: (041) 26459

Mellifont, known as 'Old Mellifont' to distinguish it from the new monastery at Collon, claims fame through being the first Cistercian house in Ireland. Although the remains are rather fragmentary in comparison to some of the country's other sites, the ruins, which stand side by side with a youth hostel, come to life once you start finding out more about their colourful history and strong influence on other monastic buildings in Ireland. The information boards and visitor's guide make fascinating reading.

The monastery was founded by St Malachy, Archbishop of Armagh, in the mid-twelfth century. Conforming to the usual layout for Cistercian houses, it was richly decorated, and took fifteen years to complete. The monks were trained by St Bernard of Clairvaux in the strict Cistercian rule of communal prayer and hard work. Mellifont became one of the most prosperous Cistercian houses in Ireland. It was also the centre of the great rebellion of the Irish houses in the early thirteenth century, holding out against interference from Anglo-Norman foundations. After the dissolution the abbey was made into a fortified residence and this was where Hugh O'Neill was starved into surrendering to Lord Deputy Mountjoy in 1603, marking the end of Gaelic Ireland. In 1690 King William had his headquarters here during the Battle of the Boyne.

Little is left standing but it is still possible to see fragments, including a few arches of the cloister, and the main outlines of the church and conventual buildings. Perhaps the most unusual of the remaining buildings is the Lavabo, a strange and now roofless structure where the monks washed their hands before mealtimes. The fourteenth-century chapter house, once used for daily meetings, has some fine carved stones and glazed tiles on display. However, it is the setting that really makes the ruins stand out. Cistercians tended to choose secluded sites for their settlements, far away from any temptation that town and city life may bring – and what could provide a more ideal setting than here on the bank of the Nattock River?

Open: May to mid-Sept, daily,
10.00–18.00
Admission charge

DROGHEDA

This historic town on the River Boyne is best explored on foot, its maze of congested streets makes driving difficult. A good Tourist Trail booklet is available which outlines a walking route around the points of interest. Drogheda began as a ford, situated where St Mary's bridge now stands between the Bull Ring and Shop Street. The Vikings first settled here in around 911 AD and the town grew into an important trading centre. In the twelfth century a bridge was built at the site of the ford and the town was divided. These two towns, continually at loggerheads, were finally united in 1412. Walled and well-fortified, Drogheda became a major port.

For the best overall view of the town head for the Millmount Martello tower set on a grassy mound believed to have been built on the grave of a son of Milesius in 1029 BC and used by the Vikings for ceremonies. From here, the whole of the walled town spreads out before you and you can fully appreciate its extent, the walls enclosing a large area of around 113 acres. Only one of the ten original thirteenth-century gates survives, **St Lawrence's Gate**, but it is remarkably well preserved. The fortifications, which were begun in 1234, remained untested until 1649 when Cromwell's troops took the town by storm, cruelly massacring some 2,000 people. The story of the bloody siege and other important events in the town's history are told through a series of exhibitions in the **Millmount House Museum** in the courtyard of the Martello tower.

Dominating the town is the splendid Victorian railway viaduct across the River Boyne. Other famous landmarks are the hospital of Our Lady of Lourdes and the old cement factory nearby. And mention must also be made of one of Drogheda's more unusual attractions which is kept in **St Peter's Church**, a modern Gothic-style church. This is where St Oliver Plunkett's head rests, a national shrine to the saint who was martyred at Tyburn in 1681. Born at Loughcrew in County Meath, he had many family connections with Drogheda.

Millmount House Museum
Tel: (041) 36391 or 31265
Open: all year, Tues–Sun,
15.00–18.00
Admission charge

St Peter's Church, West Street
Open: daily
Admission free

BOYNE VALLEY DRIVE

The road from Drogheda to the beautiful village of Slane is dotted with so many places of interest, it's well worth making the detour from the coast road and into County Meath. Just 8 km from Drogheda 'on the grassy slopes of the Boyne' is where the historic Battle of the Boyne was fought in 1690, the last time that two kings, James II of England and William of Orange, ever faced each other in battle in person. Further on is Townley Hall, a Georgian house, now a school of agriculture. The grounds have been laid out as a forest park with nature trails, scenic walks and picnic spots. This part of the River Boyne is noted for its good salmon fishing.

A left turn towards Dowth takes you past the ruins of Dowth Castle and into the area known as Bru na Boinne (Boyne Palace) in County Meath. The prehistoric passage graves of Dowth, Newgrange (see below) and Knowth, all within sight of each other, were built even before the Egyptian pyramids. In later years it is thought to have been a burial ground of the High Kings of Ireland who were crowned at the Hill of Tara. Newgrange and Dowth are open to the public, although the latter requires a great deal of energetic crawling and is of less interest to the layman than the more famous Newgrange. Knowth, which at one time had sixteen satellite tombs, is still being excavated and there is no access for visitors just yet. You can, however, see the lavish kerbstones which encircle the mound.

Further on you come to Slane with its fine Georgian houses. The village was the birthplace of the soldier-poet Francis Ledwidge, who was killed in battle at Ypres, Belgium, in 1917. Above the village rises the Hill of Slane, now a viewpoint, where St Patrick is believed to have begun the diffusion of Christianity.

Dowth
Open: June–Sept, key obtainable
Admission free

NEWGRANGE
Slane, County Meath. Tel: (041) 24488

An air of mystery shrouds this passage grave, built over 4,000 years ago by people whose only materials were stone and wood. It is a quite incredible feat of construction, made even more impressive by the fact that it is also an accurate astronomical observatory. Here, on the winter solstice, the bright rays of the rising sun hit a roof box above the entrance and filter in through a tiny slit to fill the central chamber of the tomb with a golden light. It was a symbol of hope, that spring would bring life to the land, and perhaps even that there would be life after death for the cremated bodies in the tomb.

Newgrange consists of a passage grave and chamber covered with an extensive circular mound of loose pebbles topped with a layer of white quartz stones. The mound is surrounded by a kerb of ninety-seven large slabs, some highly decorated. Entrance is by guided tour only, the guide hugely knowledgeable and most interesting. Tours leave at regular intervals from the entrance. While you wait take a look at the stone slab nearby with its splendid spiral design. This was originally the door. A visit inside Newgrange is an incredible experience not to be missed. Cold but surprisingly dry, a 19 m long passage leads to the hexagonal chamber with recesses forming the shape of a high cross. Take a close look at the geometrical carvings throughout which still confuse the experts. Be warned, however, Newgrange is not for anyone suffering from claustrophobia; the long passage is narrow and eerie.

Open: June–Sept, daily, 10.00–19.00; Oct and May, daily, 10.00–17.00 (closed 13.00–14.00); Nov–May, Tues–Sat, 10.00–17.00 (closed 13.00–14.00); Sun, 14.00–17.00

Admission charge

INDEX